MUST SEE MISSISSIPPI

MUST SEE MISSISSIPPI

50 FAVORITE PLACES

TEXT BY MARY CAROL MILLER

PHOTOGRAPHS BY MARY ROSE CARTER

INTRODUCTION BY GREG ILES

UNIVERSITY PRESS OF MISSISSIPPI / JACKSON

A Mary Jayne G. Whittington Book in the Arts

www.upress.state.ms.us

Designed by Todd Lape

The University Press of Mississippi is a member of
the Association of American University Presses.

First printing 2007
∞
Library of Congress Cataloging-in-Publication Data

Miller, Mary Carol.
Must see Mississippi : 50 favorite places / text by Mary Carol Miller ;
photographs by Mary Rose Carter. — 1st ed.
p. cm.
Includes bibliographical references and index.
ISBN-13: 978-1-57806-845-6 (cloth : alk. paper)
ISBN-10: 1-57806-845-2 (pbk. : alk. paper) 1. Mississippi—Guidebooks.
2. Historic sites—Mississippi—Guidebooks. 3. Mississippi—History, Local.
I. Carter, Mary Rose. II. Title.
F339.3.M55 2007
976.2—dc22   2007004981

British Library Cataloging-in-Publication Data available

DEDICATED TO THE MEMORY OF MICHAEL HAMMOND CARTER III

DECEMBER 19, 2005–MARCH 3, 2006

"ABUNDANT LOVE ROSE UP ABOUT HIM"

Contents

ACKNOWLEDGMENTS

We are deeply grateful to all the homeowners, curators, archivists, and local historians who provide us with access to their homes and historic sites and share their expertise, research materials, and local lore. A book such as this would never be possible without the cooperation of the people who take care of our National Register treasures each day.

Seetha Srinivasan, Craig Gill, Steve Yates, and all the staff at University Press of Mississippi have been endlessly supportive and encouraging throughout this project. Their insight and professionalism make our jobs easy and fun. Mississippi is fortunate to have University Press, one of the nation's premier academic publishers, in its corner to promote and celebrate our state, and we are fortunate to be part of this team.

And, as always, we are indebted to our families—to Jimmy and Mike, Emily and Jim, Claire, Hal, Wade and Anna, and Walker and Janet.

Our gratitude goes to those who helped us with the following sites:

Castalian Springs: Marshall Ramsey
Chamberlain-Hunt Academy: Doug Lum, Jack West
Chapel of the Cross and Chapel of the Cross Rectory: Judy Barnes
Christ Episcopal Church: Rt. Reverend A. C. Marble, Rt. Reverend Duncan Gray
Cotesworth: Katharine Williams
Clifton: Billy and Rebecca Hood, Joe Schmelzer, Dorothy Greer
DeSoto County Courthouse: Vanessa Lynchard
Eudora Welty House: Mary Alice White
Falkner-Gary House: Betty Gary
First Presbyterian Church of Port Gibson: Michael Herron
Governor's Mansion: Mary Lohrenz

Grand Village of the Natchez Indians: Jim Barnett

The Hill: Doug Lum

Jefferson College: Jim Barnett, Cheryl Branyan

L. Q. C. Lamar House: Patricia Young

Little Red Schoolhouse: Wanda Joiner, George Stafford

Monmouth: Lani Riches, Larry Stewart

Neshoba County Fairgrounds: Debbie Hall, Lavelle and
    Pat Woodrick

Oakland Chapel: Christopher Cason

Vicksburg's Old Courthouse Museum: Gordon Cotton

Port Gibson sites: Al Hollingsworth

Provine Chapel: Lewis Oswalt

Tate County Courthouse: Wayne Crockett, Gail
    Tomlinson

Temple Gemiluth Chassed: Doug Lum

Vicksburg National Military Park (Illinois Monument
    and Shirley House): Patricia Montague

Victoria: Jim Crosby

Walter Place: Jorja Lynn

Wilkinson County sites: David A. Smith

Windsor: Jim Barnett

PREFACE

More than a decade ago, we set out to photograph and research Mississippi's historic architecture. We wandered the highways and back roads from Tupelo to Woodville, from Holly Springs to Pass Christian, and found ourselves on a thousand detours in between. Our magazine articles featured everything from the witch's grave in Yazoo City to Silk Stocking Row in Aberdeen and the quiet grace of Deer Creek, winding its way through Leland.

There was more out there than could be described within the limitations of magazine space. So we expanded our horizons, setting out with the tripod, miles of film, and open minds, searching for the noteworthy and the obscure, the celebrated and the forgotten emblems of our state's history. *Written in the Bricks* highlighted fifteen towns around Mississippi, documenting their development and unique nature through their built environment. We watched Brookhaven's Lampton Auditorium and Meridian's Grand Opera House being pulled back from the very precipice of extinction, saved by local people who just refused to turn

their backs on these architectural treasures. Greenwood's Grand Boulevard offered up one outstanding house after another, all wrapped in a lush mile of towering oak trees. Ocean Springs and Pass Christian were jewels of seaside ease, their denizens sending us on our way with sympathy that we didn't have the wisdom, or the good fortune, to sit with them and watch those sunsets over the gulf each evening.

Written in the Bricks was bookended by two retrospective reviews of architectural history, *Lost Mansions of Mississippi* and *Lost Landmarks of Mississippi*. Those were primarily Mary Carol's work, with archival illustrations, but the two most poignant photos in the series were taken through Mary Rose's lens. In the *Lost Mansions* frontispiece, the Grove's columns stand silently in a Wilkinson County forest, eerily reminiscent of the better-known Windsor. They've been there for over a century, and the house that they once fronted retreats further into memory with each passing year and generation. Mary Rose's photograph, taken on a barren winter's day, captures the magnitude of our loss each time one of these irreplaceable homes is lost to fire or neglect. An equally striking photo is the cover shot from *Lost Landmarks*. The afternoon sun angles through the bleak but beautiful ruins of St. John's Episcopal Church, highlighting the delicate arches and rose windows fashioned by a talented slave artisan before the Civil War.

Those forays into Mississippi's vanished architecture fired our determination to capture what's left. *Great Houses of Mississippi* featured thirty-five of the region's finest antebellum homes, ranging from the staid Federal mansions of Natchez to the wildly exuberant facades of Longwood and Walter Place. For two devotees of Mississippi's past, it was the chance of a lifetime to explore the best of our heritage. We lugged camera equipment to the top of Longwood's dusty, echoing floors. Up there, sixty feet above the first level, nothing separated us from empty space except a disturbingly thin rail. It was worth it, though, to experience what Haller Nutt must have felt in the 1860s, as he wandered his doomed mansion and felt his dreams evaporate along with the future of the South. Two hundred miles upriver, we worried for the fate of Mount Holly, as the winds off Lake Washington crept through its broken windows and its curved arches gave way to gravity.

Most visits were more hopeful. Preservationists at Rosedale demonstrated their newest technology, digitally peeling away untold layers of paint to reveal the colors originally laid down by W. W. Topp in the 1850s. And at Riverview we witnessed the ingenuity of a long-forgotten craftsman who had glazed the cupola in multicolored glass panes. When the morning sun's rays line up just right, they cast a rainbow down the curved stairway. That's happened on every cloudless day for fifteen decades, and we were just privileged to be there to enjoy it in 2003.

In the course of our travels for these books, we never failed to stumble across numerous outstanding examples of historic Mississippi architecture. While the white-columned mansion in the midst of a cotton field may be the iconic image of the "Old South," it overshadows a vast array of churches, college buildings, memorials, and public structures. Having spent two years concentrating on those white columns and the great houses they support, we wanted to shift gears and tell the story of the myriad architectural treasures scattered throughout the state. There are literally thousands, many of which are listed on the National Register of Historic Places. We used that collection as a rough framework for our choices in this collection, and all but a handful of the sites you will find here are recognized on the National Register. Several, including Grand Village, Monmouth, Oakland Chapel, the Governor's Mansion, the Old Capitol, the Eudora Welty House, the L. Q. C. Lamar House, and Vicksburg's Old Courthouse Museum, have achieved an even more privileged designation as National Historic Landmarks.

The obvious question concerns how we chose the fifty sites that are included. As always, we tried to be geographically diverse, recognizing that the lonely Jacinto Courthouse in Rienzi tells a tale just as vividly as the storm-battered Our Lady of the Gulf Catholic Church in Bay St. Louis. Historic treasures are found in downtown Jackson as well as in tiny Glen Allan and isolated Tishomingo State Park. We drew from a wide array of styles and periods, ranging from the ageless paths of the Old Natchez Trace to

Eudora Welty's 1920s Tudor home in Belhaven. The lively mix of cultures in Mississippi is represented by structures as different as the Greek Revival homes of antebellum leaders L. Q. C. Lamar and John Quitman, the ruins of historically black Mississippi Industrial College in Holly Springs, and the haunting mounds at Grand Village of the Natchez Indians. Churches run the gamut from the Gothic Episcopal chapels at Mannsdale and Church Hill to the incongruent Temple Gemiluth Chassed in Port Gibson. Several of the most outstanding buildings in the state were designed for education, including William Nichols's Lyceum at Ole Miss and Oakland Chapel at Alcorn State University.

Our goal was to tell the stories and highlight the beauty of both the vaunted sites, known to every tourist and aficionado of southern history, and those tucked-away places that only the locals can find. Where else but in Mississippi would you find Hernando's mayor bumping down old Highway 51 with a truck full of discarded canvas masterpieces, or see the handiwork of an army of talented Japanese gardeners reclaimed from the kudzu-covered gullies of Marshall County? Aberdeen boasts a Victorian jewel of a house, once crumbling around a sightless spinster and unwanted by her heirs, now restored to its original grandeur. In Vicksburg's military park, a marble and granite memorial to thousands of scared-stiff Illinois soldiers rose from a battle-scarred hillside even as Mississippi's lawmakers debated the state's obligation to memorialize its own lost generation. Every county and every town has its own quirky architectural prize, waiting to be discovered and enjoyed.

One further note of explanation is appropriate regarding our choices. The idea for this book evolved over the course of a very long, very late drive from Pass Christian to Jackson in December 2004. We had participated in a Christmas festival and book signing in the Pass, surrounded by the Christmas lights strung along the verandas of Scenic Drive's antebellum mansions and up the masts of the ships at the Yacht Club. We all know that hurricanes and wild weather are a predictable peril of life in such an idyllic spot, but no one could have anticipated the devastation that would descend on that lovely community and its neighbors just a few months later. The entire list of coastal sites that we discussed on that drive north from the gulf were either obliterated or mangled beyond recognition in a matter of a few hours on August 29, 2005. We waited for almost a year after Katrina before venturing down to take pictures, and found three sites which we felt represented the courageous rebuilding that is under way from Bay St. Louis to Pascagoula. While struggling to replace their own homes, our friends on the coast have also poured their hearts into saving what remains of their historic sites, and we admire them for their determination and attitude.

So here's our very eclectic collection of Mississippi's best, and our favorites, gleaned from many days on the road and suggestions from throughout the state. It is our hope that readers will enjoy this selection and be inspired to visit these sites, to be mindful of the worthwhile places in their own communities, and to join in the ongoing effort to preserve our shared architectural heritage.

INTRODUCTION

When I first heard about Einstein's theory of relativity and its implications for time, I had no trouble accepting these ideas, though I was only a boy. After all, I lived in Mississippi, a state that constantly fluctuated in the temporal dimension, staying ten to fifteen years behind the rest of America in most things. New haircuts, music, and trendy fashions always arrived late, after they had become mainstream elsewhere, and some cultural touchstones never arrived at all. Certain films never played in Mississippi, as though they had been made in an alternate universe and could not be shipped here. Great music that was moving the rest of the country didn't play on our radio stations, though some of it was being made by Mississippi-born artists. Certain novels weren't taught in our schools, and more ominously, some laws didn't seem to apply here. Modern architecture was as alien to me as props from a science fiction movie. It was as though, culturally speaking, I lived in a different dimension than the kids growing up in California and New York, or even in Ohio. Mississippi stood outside historical time as I understood it, even as history began to happen here, and the attention of the world focused on us.

In Natchez, I grew up not merely in the shadow of history, but in the cloistered heart of it, in a veritable time capsule. Not only had the great antebellum houses of my city been lovingly preserved, but also many of her social mores and rituals. Childhood in this insular world had both dark and light sides. I dug up arrowheads in the sandy creeks where Natchez Indians had walked before me, and was fired with a curiosity about history stretching eons back before the provincial "history" celebrated every March in my town. While the civil rights struggle raged in my backyard, I dressed in velvet breeches and Confederate uniforms, learned to bow and to waltz with ladies fifty years my senior. My pageant clothes were cleaned and pressed by a black housekeeper who loved me like a son and taught me more about life than most. This almost surreal upbringing was probably a fortuitous beginning for a southern writer, for it taught me early about the contradictions prevalent in my native region and, I would later learn, in America as a whole.

I have written often of Mississippi, but when I was asked to write an introduction to this book, I suspected that a mistake had been made. Having spent most of my years in Natchez, I felt that my knowledge was insufficient to add anything of merit to a volume of photographs and prose that encompassed the entire state. It must be a rule of human nature that when you are from a place, even a famous one, you don't pay much attention to its wonders. It's not that familiarity breeds contempt, exactly, but it does tend to make one take things for granted. I figure most Egyptian kids raised in the shadow of the pyramids look at the great tombs as a way to make money off the tourists, not as awe-inspiring marvels. I was reared fifty feet from the wrought-iron fence that encircles Oakland, the mansion that served as a hotel for Union officers in Natchez during the Civil War. Every spring, this historic house seemed to float on a pink ocean of azaleas, yet to me and my friends it was merely a setting for the game of "army," the greatest pretend-wartime theater of operations any boy could desire. One buddy made still more utilitarian use of Oakland, by informing the Yankee tourists who flocked to our neighborhood that they had to pay a fee of one dollar per car for the privilege of parking on our street. This bit of sharp practice was soon uncovered (and terminated), but it confirms my thesis that natives are not always the best appreciators of the treasures in their midst.

Despite my misgivings about my qualifications, I decided to look at the manuscript of this book. After only a few pages I discovered that it was not exactly what I had expected. *Must See Mississippi* is not the "obvious" book on Mississippi architecture and the history behind it. The authors have produced several works prior to this, and those volumes chronicle the iconic "Old South" architecture that springs to mind when the average tourist hears the word "Mississippi." This book is a record of more subtle treasures, those likely to be missed on a first or even second journey to our state.

As I perused the entries in this book, I realized that I had personal connections to more than a few buildings in it. I actually caught my breath when I turned the page and saw the Falkner-Gary house on Buchanan Street in Oxford. The text described not only this house, but a little building behind it known as Mammy Callie's cabin. As a boy, William Faulkner sat in this cabin for many hours and listened to the family's black housekeeper tell tales of the secret history of Lafayette County. I happen to know that another Mississippi writer spent quite a bit of time in Mammy Callie's cabin as well. For two years during my sojourn at Ole Miss, I lived in those two modest rooms, renting from Knox and Betty Gary, who had restored the main house in the 1970s. The occupancy of the cabin was passed down to me (with some sense of ceremony) by fellow Natchezian Win Ward, who also dreamed of becoming a writer and who is today a noted Mississippi attorney. On the day I moved in Win told me that Faulkner had "played in the cabin as a child," but I assumed this was more legend than truth, likely exaggerated by the new owners. And yet . . . while I lived in Mammy Callie's cabin, surrounded by the somnolent oaks of Oxford, I sensed a presence that I cannot quite describe. My best explanation is that in that cabin I never felt quite alone.

At this time I was studying under Willie Morris, who was then writer-in-residence at Ole Miss. Though not yet writing fiction myself, I was greedily devouring thousands of pages of it, and listening to lectures by William Styron, James Dickey, John Knowles, and other of Willie's literary friends. At the time, I didn't quite grasp the romance of all this, but looking back, I see how intense a time it was. The certainty that I would one day write my own novels began to crystallize in those two rooms. But it took reading *Must See Mississippi* twenty-seven years later to confirm the legend that for years I had secretly hoped was true: Old Bill and I had shared the same physical space, even if he was a very young Bill at the time. And wasn't it Faulkner, after all, who in his most overquoted statement told the *Paris Review* that "the past is not dead, it's not even past"? *Perhaps*, I thought after reading this section of the book, *I absorbed a wisp of the magic that Mammy Callie and Faulkner left lingering behind them. And perhaps I know more about the buildings in this book than I thought.*

One fact cannot be escaped when reading *Must See Mississippi*. In these pages we are looking at the past. Scholars do not drive the scenic back roads—or even the city thoroughfares—of Mississippi to chronicle cutting-edge architecture. Mississippi is not merely of the past; it *is* the past. For here survives a way of life that has mostly vanished elsewhere. Willie Morris used to say that the South is primarily about remembrance. In many ways, the South—and more particularly Mississippi—is the memory of our nation. The cardinal American virtues that once thrived in every state in the union still pulse with life here. Jonathan Yardley once enumerated those virtues as: "Love for and closeness to the land; a strong and intimate sense of family; an awareness of the past and its hard lessons; genuine hospitality, civility, and courtliness; perhaps most of all, a sense of community. . . ." It's quite common to find four generations of a Mississippi family living in the same town, and sometimes more. In *Must See Mississippi*, we find many of the public buildings that served those families in their daily lives, and in some cases still do. There are churches, courthouses, and schools, along with fairgrounds, a lighthouse, a swinging bridge, and even Miss Eudora's house in Belhaven. All have endured through many long decades, some, like the columns of Windsor, by sheer strength, and others, like the Biloxi lighthouse, by divine providence. But most have survived because of the dedicated efforts of Mississippians bent on preserving what they could of their past.

In our present politically correct climate, some question the value of saving symbols of the Old South. After all, the South is bound inextricably with the ancient sin of slavery and was almost destroyed because of it. Some buildings in this book were actually constructed by the hands of slaves; the rest were erected when equality for black Americans was still a distant dream (and some say it still is). But do we throw out the Declaration of Independence because Thomas Jefferson owned slaves? Human beings are creatures of paradox, and history is rife with the irony of contradictory actions carried out by the same man, state, or nation. Ancient Egypt was a slave state, but no one questions the morality of preserving the pyramids. *Must See Mississippi* does not seek to celebrate Old South Mississippi so much as to present and explain it. Mary Carol Miller's text illuminates Mary Rose Carter's fine photographs with scholarly historical detachment, yet in her anecdotes about the people behind these places, I sense a strong partisanship for her material.

I understand her feelings well.

While most communities in America seem hell-bent on turning themselves into clones of the next city up the interstate, Mississippi remains true to itself. All around us, developers work ceaselessly to throw up the same haphazard collection of buildings: Wal-Mart and Pottery Barn and Old Navy, Circuit City and Home Depot and Bonefish Grill. Even Deep South stalwarts like Georgia and Alabama are falling prey to this mass homogenization. But Mississippi still resists this culturally lethal virus. Mississippi towns are stubborn in their uniqueness, clinging to their individuality like Flannery O'Connor characters. Some might say there's simply not enough money to be made here to draw the big franchises, and maybe that's true.

Maybe that's the way we like it.

I don't want every town I visit to look the same. I don't want to eat the same reheated frozen food at the same restaurant with the same chain stores staring back at me through the window. America never was about everyone and everything being the same. America was born from the human desire to be free, and true liberty means having the freedom to be different. In Mississippi we still are. One pass through this book will tell you that. We wake up and go to work or play in a world filled with talismans from the past. Their importance is not that they tie us to the politics of the past, or to the sins of history. They tie us to our ancestors—to our dead—and to the land that bore us all. They anchor us in time, telling us who we were and, by extension, who we are becoming.

I have written that Mississippi is the past, and this is true. But Mississippi isn't *only* the past. It may also hold the secret to the future for all Americans. While cities around the country become ever more homogenous in appearance, they also, through immigration, become more ethnically diverse. But in Mississippi we're still basically black and white (with a few Native Americans and others in the mix). And when people talk about race in America today, they're talking about black and white. This is the fundamental disconnect in our society, the wound in the side of the American dream.

The answer to our national identity crisis may well lie in Mississippi. The great racial tragedies of America played themselves out on our soil. The Indians were in Mississippi before us, and we wiped out their culture. The Africans who survived the infamous Middle Passage were brought here by the thousands, and lived and died along the great river until Mississippi became as much a part of their collective soul as ours. The music they made here mourned and celebrated the multifold mystery that was Mississippi better than we could do it ourselves. We sent thousands of boys to die in a misguided cause, struggled through Reconstruction and the 1960s, and still somehow survived as a biracial society, with one foot in the past and the other probing hesitantly into the future. Now we sit at the bottom of the list of states in most things. Education. Employment. Wages. Manufacturing. High technology.

But we are not lost.

We know who we are. We know this, because we haven't forgotten where we came from, or how we got here. A lot of us still live on the same land our ancestors did. People who fled this state decades ago in anger or fear are returning in numbers, many of them to stay. Why? Because most Southern expatriates still live here in their minds, no matter how far they might run to escape the state that they believed was their problem. You cannot escape Mississippi. If you are born here, reared here, the place insinuates itself into every living cell (a spiritual osmosis possibly driven by the god-awful humidity), then replicates itself endlessly, for there is no cure for being from Mississippi. Our peculiarly contagious identity has swept across the country and around the world, carried in our prolific music and literature, changing the course of American culture and even that of the world. Why? Because Mississippi, for all its flaws, is the real deal. Mississippians live in intimate proximity to the primeval sources of life, the land and the river. Life here is intricately woven from the old verities that Faulkner held dear: love and honor and pity and pride and compassion and sacrifice. Perhaps most important, we live at the nexus between the black race and the white.

The great truth about Mississippi is this: almost nothing is hidden. Hypocrisy is not our way. Despite its rhetoric, the North has also always been segregated, by money and by class and by race. But in the South, where segregation was open, we were all in it together. Three bad years in a row for farmers affected everybody, black and white. It just hit the black people quicker and harder. My "insular" world was filled with people, black and white, living and working elbow-to-elbow, interacting every day, trying to find their way through the crazy world they had been born into.

I recognize the inequalities of my upbringing. The kids I played army with on the grounds of Oakland were all white. When integration came to our town in 1969, my parents waited only one semester before moving me to a parochial (and all-white) school. They were moderates and claimed they moved me because the quality of education was bound to suffer in those times, and it inarguably did. But the prospects for true change suffered too, and Mississippi was left with a fractured educational system that handicaps us to this day. A lot of water has gone under the bridge since then, most of it muddy and some of it bloody. But the thing that gives me hope is this: here in the belly of the beast, in benighted and atavistic old Mississippi, things have changed for the better.

How do I know?

For those who demand irrefutable evidence of change, I suggest a visit to an unlikely place: the Dixie Youth baseball fields of Natchez's Duncan Park, named after the most prosperous cotton planter and slaveholder of the 1850s. Here my nine-year-old son plays baseball with black and white kids alike, some under the direction of black coaches, something unthinkable not so long ago. Now and then I stand quietly in the dugout and marvel at the change that only time (and the death of some) could bring about.

We still have a long way to go; only a fool would dispute that. But the ground still left to cover is more economic than moral. We know how to live together here. In some ways, we always have. From Mississippi, we look out at the greater country and see confusion, a vacuous culture of the moment, and no clear compass guiding us into the future. We don't want to return to the past, but to preserve what was best about it. We have always sensed that America as a whole was losing its way. In *Dixie Rising*, Peter Applebome of the *New York Times* points out the many ways in which America, in its recent search for a firm identity, has embraced many aspects of southern culture. A lot of Americans, quite simply, are trying to find their way back to where we have always been. Applebome concludes: "We would all be worse off if in our admirable rush to extinguish forever the South's ancient sins, we end up burying its enduring virtues as well."

Must See Mississippi is an immensely readable historical guide to some of the buildings and spaces that shaped Mississippians of the past, and also contemporary Mississippians like me. You won't find the complete history of every building in this book. No writer could ever discover the secret significance of structures and sites to the people who built them, who inhabit them, or who simply pass through them. As a boy, I helped to clean Christ Episcopal Church; it was one of the duties of belonging to Trinity Episcopal Church in those days. A few years later, I rode a rickety old school bus to play football against the notoriously tough young men of Chamberlain-Hunt

Academy. In 1977, I stood on the steps of the Old Capitol as a delegate to Boys' State. A year later, I registered for my Ole Miss classes in the basement of the Lyceum. I began to find my path as a writer in Mammy Callie's cabin behind the Falkner-Gary House, and I wandered the haunted ruins of Windsor with a girl almost as beautiful as Elizabeth Taylor in *Raintree County*. I was initiated into my fraternity in the basement of First Presbyterian Church in Oxford. And in 1980 I heard Ronald Reagan give a presidential campaign speech at the Neshoba County Fairgrounds. Reading *Must See Mississippi* taught me something I didn't know about each of these places. So turn the page and discover, or rediscover, some of the lesser-known jewels that make Mississippi the most unique and emotionally vibrant state in the Union.

It's well worth the trip.

—GREG ILES

MUST SEE MISSISSIPPI

GRAND VILLAGE OF THE NATCHEZ INDIANS

NATCHEZ IS WORLD RENOWNED for its antebellum architecture and tales of nineteenth-century cotton millionaires. It has the highest concentration of historic properties in Mississippi, and each year attracts thousands of tourists who flock to see two-hundred-year-old mansions like Rosalie, Auburn, and Monmouth.

Most of those visitors never realize that, right within the city limits of Natchez, are remnants of a culture that is far older than that found in the pilgrimage sites. Grand Village holds just a hint of the Natchez Indians, who may have been the last survivors of the prehistoric Mississippi Culture and who dominated life in the southeastern United States from approximately A.D. 1000 to the time of the first European explorers. The Natchez, unlike the nearby Choctaws and Chickasaws, had a theocratic system that revolved around a Great Sun leader and mound building. Their oral tradition held that they had migrated from Mexico into the area that would one day be Mississippi. At their peak, there may have been two hundred thousand tribal members, ruled over by nineteen hundred Suns.

When Hernando de Soto's expedition sailed down the Mississippi River in 1541, they were relentlessly attacked by warriors under the direction of Chief Quigaltanqu. This chieftain was most likely a Natchez Indian. The French explorer La Salle arrived in the region 140 years later, and found a collection of nine villages scattered along St. Catherine's Creek. The largest and most well developed was Grand Village, which included the home of the Great Sun.

The Great Sun was a theocratic and all-powerful ruler of his people, a member of the highest Sun Class in Natchez hierarchy. Just beneath that class were the Nobles and the Honored People; at the bottom were the Stinkards, or common people. The sister of the Great Sun held an honored position within the tribe, and it was through her son that succession was achieved. At the Great Sun's death, family members and other important

members of the community were strangled to accompany him in the afterlife.

The Great Sun's home was built on a huge raised mound. The most important structure in Grand Village would have been the thirty-foot-high sacred temple, site of a continuously burning fire. Four warriors were assigned to keep this flame burning; extinction of the flame meant death for them.

In the decades between the arrival of de Soto's troops and the appearance of La Salle, diseases had decimated the Natchez. By the time the first provincial French outpost was established on the Mississippi River bluffs in 1713, the remaining Indians had clustered in their little villages along St. Catherine's Creek. One of the French settlers described his impression:

> The Village of the Natchez is the most beautiful that could be found in Louisiana. It is beautified by very pretty walks which nature, and not artifice, has formed there. Around it are flower-adorned prairies, broken by little hills upon which there are thickets of all kinds of fragrant trees. Several little streams of very clear water issue from beneath a mountain visible for two leagues across the prairies and, after watering them in many places, they gather up into two big creeks which encircle the village, beyond which they unite in the form of a small river which flows over very fine gravel

Left: Early French explorers would have encountered Natchez Indian huts similar to this reproduction at Grand Village.

Right: The Natchez Indians' sacred temple, lit by a continuously burning flame, was centered on this raised mound.

and passes on . . . into the Missicipy [*sic*] . . . All the necessities of life are here, such as buffaloes, cows, deer, chickens and turkeys and an abundance of geese. There are also fish in abundance . . . As for fruit there is more than any other place in Louisiana.[1]

For obvious reasons, the French were attracted to such a fine site, and by 1716 they had erected palisaded Fort Rosalie on the bluffs high above the Mississippi River. Tensions were inevitable with the Natchez, whose villages surrounded the fort. Petty thievery and resentment of intermarriage between French settlers and Indians simmered for more than a decade.

In 1729, the tactless Fort Rosalie commander, Sieur de Chepart, demanded tribute from the Great Sun and relinquishment of either Grand Village or nearby White Apple Village for his personal use. The Natchez were insulted and furious. The Great Sun called for a coordinated strike against the French, allying his own warriors with neighboring Choctaws and Yazoos. Bundles of sticks were handed to each tribe, with instructions to subtract one stick per day and anticipate war when the sticks were gone. The Choctaws and Yazoos followed the plan, but the Great Sun's mother sabotaged the bundle held by the Natchez. She may have been married to a Frenchman; when Chepart ignored her warnings of an imminent attack, she hid several of her son's sticks, sending the Natchez into a premature battle.

In spite of her treachery, the Natchez were victorious over the unsuspecting French garrison. Several hundred soldiers were massacred and dozens of women and children taken hostage. A few months later, the French retaliated, aided by the Choctaws. The Natchez were all but destroyed. Those who survived were rounded up and sold into slavery. A few escaped across the river to Louisiana and were likely amalgamated into other tribes who wound up in Oklahoma.

Grand Village was slowly surrounded by the growing city of Natchez, with no visible reminders of the once-thriving ancient culture except the abandoned mounds. The first major archeological excavations were carried out in the 1930s, and the State of Mississippi assumed control of the site in 1976.

OLD NATCHEZ TRACE

WHEN FEDERAL TROOPS MARCHED northward from Bruinsburg in the spring of 1863, one of the largest towns they encountered was Rocky Springs, Mississippi. Several thousand people made their homes here, utilizing the Methodist church, post office, schools, Masonic Lodge, and stores. Its origins stretched back to the days when the Natchez Trace was the primary route through the Mississippi wilderness between Natchez and Nashville.

The forty thousand soldiers who camped in and around Rocky Springs did the town little if any damage, but their presence was the first of a series of man-made and natural disasters that would doom the town. Fifteen years after those soldiers headed off to Vicksburg, a yellow fever epidemic decimated the community. The once-lush cotton fields that surrounded Rocky Springs were depleted of topsoil and rapidly eroded into frightening, weed-choked gullies. When the boll weevil crept in at the turn of the twentieth century, there was no hope. One by one, the remaining families moved on, and the once-bustling buildings collapsed into the creeping undergrowth.

At the Rocky Springs rest stop and campground on the modern Natchez Trace, all that remains of the town are the Methodist church, its graveyard, and an old safe found deep in the woods. Nearby are several of the more well-preserved sections of the original sunken Trace, worn down by centuries of erosion and thousands of feet and hooves.

Before the arrival of European settlers in the Mississippi valley, Choctaws and Chickasaws had established villages in what would one day be the Magnolia State. An informal network of trails linked the Indian towns, and those trails would prove invaluable to white pioneers in the late 1700s. British explorers in the 1760s drew maps of the region, with the Trace roughly outlined as "Path to the Choctaw Nation."

As Natchez developed into a prosperous Mississippi River port, it attracted thousands of flatboats, which would

float down the Ohio and Mississippi rivers with produce and finished goods. The crews would tie up at Natchez, carouse for a while under the bluffs, and then begin the long trek on foot back to Nashville and points north. They followed the rough Indian trails that the French labeled "tracier," meaning track or course.

Over approximately a forty-year span, thousands of boatmen, pioneers, peddlers, and preachers would walk or ride the Trace, tramping down the earth until, in many places, the road was sunken several feet beneath the surrounding countryside. It was often a dark, dangerous journey, with few way stations and no lawmen to protect travelers from bandits and thugs.

Although no one could foresee it at the time, 1811 would be the year that the Trace began to die. Robert Fulton had perfected his model of a steam-powered boat, and Nicholas Roosevelt piloted the three-hundred-ton *New Orleans* down the Ohio River, into the Mississippi and straight into the maelstrom of the New Madrid earthquake. When the ship finally tied up at Natchez, it caused an immediate commotion. The crew didn't break their boat apart and set out on foot, as their predecessors had, but simply got back on, reversed the engines, and headed back upstream.

Over the next few years, traffic on the Natchez Trace dwindled to almost nothing. It lapsed into legend, and with increased development all along its route from Natchez to Nashville, the path gradually disappeared. It

Left: Rocky Springs Methodist Church is the lone remaining structure in the lost Claiborne County community.

Right: Centuries of use by Native Americans and pioneers wore the soft dirt of the Natchez Trace into sunken tunnels.

would take the dogged determination of a Virginia native, Elizabeth Blanton Jones, to save the memory of the Trace. This Holly Springs matron, first state regent of the Mississippi Daughters of the American Revolution, organized a plan to place commemorative boulders in every county of Mississippi, Alabama, and Tennessee through which the Trace had passed. She laid the first marker in Natchez in 1909 and set out to be sure every county participated. Mississippi's First Lady, Mrs. Edmund Noel, marveled at the tenacity of Elizabeth Jones: "We have one dreamer . . . who can see the Natchez Trace restored and become a great artery of commerce. Along the highway our dreamer also sees magnolias planted . . . I must say it takes 'an eye of faith' to see our county supervisors giving proper attention to road making, much less landscape

gardening . . . but all ideas are slow of accomplishment, and we, the committee, pray that faith even as a 'grain of mustard seed' . . . may cause our successors to preserve, and in the far future, perhaps, accomplish the work begun by the Daughters of the American Revolution."[2]

Mrs. Noel had no notion of just how extreme the "far future" was going to be. Another quarter century would elapse before federal aid came to the Natchez Trace project. Congressman Thomas Jefferson Busby petitioned President Franklin Roosevelt with a proposal to survey the old Trace and build a modern road along its course. Busby not only valued the road for its historic significance, but envisioned thousands of construction and maintenance jobs arising from the Depression-era project. Desperately needing the good will of the Senate finance chairman, Mississippi's Pat Harrison, Roosevelt pushed the bill through Congress and told Secretary of the Interior Harold Ickes to find the funds. Ickes was adamantly opposed to the project, but he bowed to Roosevelt's wishes and freed up $1.2 million for initial costs.

The first contracts for Natchez Trace construction were let in June 1937. Construction stopped and started for decades, leaving motorists zigging and zagging on and off the road as it disappeared for miles at a time. Finally, on May 21, 2005, the last ribbon was cut, and the Natchez Trace Parkway was open for its entire 444-mile length. Acknowledged as one of America's most scenic byways, its smooth asphalt belies the tortuous journey the Trace once entailed. In just a few spots, such as Rocky Springs, travelers with time to explore can rediscover stretches of the dark and treacherous sunken road through the wilderness.

Hanging moss and ancient cedars surround the grave markers behind Rocky Springs Methodist Church.

Monmouth

MOST OF THE GREAT ANTEBELLUM mansions of Natchez and the southwest corner of Mississippi reflect a degree of detail and filigree that can readily be perceived as feminine and fanciful, in spite of their dominating size. Monmouth, on the other hand, is a notable exception, with its unmistakably masculine facade and sheer heaviness. It mirrors the personality of the man who purchased it in 1826 and remade it to suit his tastes.

Natchez postmaster John Hankinson hired an architect, possibly Levi Weeks, to build his house in 1818. Federal patronage jobs must have been lucrative, for Hankinson's home was an impressive two-story brick Federal-style structure with a cellar, a detached kitchen, a garden house, and functional outbuildings. Details included marble keystones over the windows and a doorway flanked by narrow windows rather than sidelights. Hankinson lived there until his death in 1824. The property was auctioned off two years later to John Anthony Quitman, a rising star in Natchez society.

Quitman, born in New York and educated in Ohio, was determined to make his fortune in the prosperous new state of Mississippi. He stepped off a boat at Natchez Under-the-Hill in 1821 and soon after opened a law office in the booming river town. Accumulating clients and land, he was also ardently courting Eliza Turner, niece of one of the county's most prominent judges. Their marriage raised him several rungs on the social ladder, but Eliza's family was wary enough to have him sign a prenuptial agreement.

It didn't take long for John Quitman to show the Natchez nabobs that he was worthy of their acceptance. After buying Monmouth, he rapidly acquired four plantations scattered around Mississippi and Louisiana. Palmyra, near Vicksburg, grew twenty-five hundred acres of cotton. Live Oaks, his Louisiana place, was a sugarcane operation. Springfield, in north Adams County, supplied the Quitman household with cattle, dairy products, and more cotton. Belen was his primitive plantation in

faraway Holmes County. All told, on his five landholdings, Quitman owned over four hundred slaves and fifteen thousand acres, making him one of the most dominant businessmen in Mississippi.

A contemporary who knew Quitman well stated that "a more ambitious man never lived."[3] He ran for and was elected to the state legislature, served on the state appeals court, and won appointment as a brigadier general in the United States Army. Lauded for his heroics in the Mexican War and having served as provisional governor of Mexico City in 1847–48, he returned to Monmouth a national hero.

Despite support for Quitman as the Democratic vice presidential nominee in 1848, he was not interested in national politics. Mississippi was his chosen home and it was there that he wielded an enormous amount of clout. He won the governor's race in 1849 and used the platform to rail against Congress's Compromise of 1850 and any encroachment on states' rights. Slavery advocates nearly pulled him into a Cuban revolutionary scheme, with the hopes that the island would become a slaveholding stalwart for the South. Believing that Mississippi and other southern states would soon be opting for secession, Quitman declined. That was a fortunate day for Mississippi's historic architecture, for Quitman turned his considerable fortune and energy toward remodeling Monmouth.

The mansion had served as General Quitman's psychological refuge since he purchased it in 1826. He doted

Page 11: Statuary, ponds, and thousands of flowering plants surround the main house and outbuildings of Monmouth.

Left: General John Anthony Quitman transformed an 1818 Federal-style mansion into one of the most imposing Greek Revival houses in Natchez.

Right: Monmouth's acres of gardens reflect Quitman's horticultural interests.

on the acres of gardens and fruit trees, planting melons, strawberries, seven varieties of peaches, ten strains of pear trees, and innumerable flowers. Mrs. Quitman wrote to one of their children that "Father has returned to his old habits and occupation of gardening and pruning trees—he in fact lives in the garden."[4]

Quitman devoted no less attention to his house than to his gardens. He hired Cincinnati architect James McClure to revamp the Federal facades into the more popular Greek Revival, in keeping with the current fashion of 1853 Natchez. A massive formal portico was added, having giant square columns of plastered brick with molded bases and caps. The columns hold up a full entablature with the classical elements of architrave, frieze, and cornice, crowned with a triangular pediment. An unusual zigzag balustrade outlines the second-floor balcony. A rear wing was added along the east side of the house, housing Quitman's library and sev-

eral bedrooms. Across the backyard, a matching two-story servants' house completes the "U-shaped" effect.

The interior of Monmouth reflects the usual floor plan of the day. A central hallway separates the parlor and drawing room on the west side from the formal and family dining rooms on the east side. A curving stairway leads up to another wide hallway and four bedrooms. The house is rich in interior detail, with fluted pilasters, marble mantels, and ceiling medallions.

The American minister to Spain, on visiting Monmouth in 1855, was impressed with the ambience of the grounds, the house, and its inhabitants: "The General's place is very striking—very much improved, yet left so as to give the most natural effect & the beautiful ground & splendid oaks, with long hanging moss, to their branches— He lives in princely style—in a castle of a house—plain and rich—old-fashioned—with very plain but rich furniture. He is immensely rich."[5]

He was immensely rich, but those fortunes couldn't save General Quitman when he contracted a mysterious illness in 1857. In what may have been a forerunner of a Legionnaire's disease–like outbreak affecting several national political figures, he became ill while visiting the National Hotel in Washington, D.C., and died a few months later.

Their patriarch's well-known secessionist ardor brought grief to Quitman's family during the Civil War. After Natchez surrendered without a fight, Union officers commandeered Monmouth, forcing the family into upstairs seclusion. Troop tents carpeted the lawn, and soldiers tramped through General Quitman's beloved gardens. A Wisconsin trooper recalled the scene in later years: "The Quitmans, like most southern people of their rank who lived out of town, kept up a garden of several acres. It contained all sorts of things from onions and potatoes to pineapples, pomegranates, figs and large pecan-nut trees . . . We used to like to walk in that garden. Its close proximity to our camp enabled us now and then to get a taste of something delicious."[6]

Those were the more benign intruders. Other soldiers ripped furniture and maliciously destroyed family heirlooms before General Henry Slocum stepped in and restored Monmouth to the Quitman family. The house stayed in their possession until 1909, when it was sold to the first of a series of owners. It was purchased by Ron and Lani Riches in 1978. They undertook a careful renovation of the aging property, complete with archeological restoration of long-lost slave quarters. Monmouth is now one of the most authentically preserved homes in Natchez, welcoming thousands of guests each year in its new role as a bed-and-breakfast inn.

Quitman added a rear wing and a two-story servants' house to Monmouth, creating a U-shaped courtyard.

JEFFERSON COLLEGE

In the six decades stretching from 1802 to 1860, Mississippi's territorial and state legislatures granted charters to thirty-two colleges. These ranged from fly-by-night religious schools which never actually opened to legitimate centers of education offering scientific, classical, and practical training. Only three have survived to the present day. Hampstead Academy evolved into Mississippi College, Centenary College relocated to Louisiana, and the University of Mississippi survived as the state's flagship institution.

Most of these short-lived colleges were no more than glorified high schools, vanishing after a few years with no architectural legacy. Several were destroyed during the Civil War, including Corinth's Corona College and Holly Springs Female Institute. A handful survived into the twentieth century, such as Grenada College, Chickasaw College, and Whitworth. They eventually succumbed to competition from community colleges and the expanding state university system.

The very first school to be chartered in Mississippi, fifteen years before statehood, was Jefferson College. The checkered history of this school reflects the antebellum struggle of a few governors and legislators to provide more than the most rudimentary of educational opportunities to the state's young people.

Mississippi was a burgeoning territory when Governor W. C. C. Claiborne presented the legislature with a proposal for a "seminary of learning." Met with the enthusiasm of high expectations, the bill sailed through the 1802 legislative session and landed on his desk on May 13 of that year. Thirty-four distinguished men were appointed to the board of the ambitiously named Jefferson College, and they held their first meeting in January of 1803.

Hopes for the quick establishment of the new school were soon dashed. In a depressing prelude to decades of educational shortsightedness, the board fractured into quarreling factions, squabbling over funding issues and

potential sites. With no money provided by the legislature, inane schemes ruled the day. A lottery garnered only a handful of ticket sales. Sections of land were earmarked for sale to generate money; unfortunately, they were in Lowndes County, which had no citizens. Frustrated and angry, the board members disbanded, and Jefferson College existed only on paper.

In 1810, after eight long years of inertia, Governor David Holmes lit a fire under the dormant college board. Jefferson College finally creaked open the next year, albeit as a preparatory school with no collegiate-level courses. With the opening of nearby Elizabeth Female Academy, its coeds withdrew, cutting the student body in half. There were no buildings, few faculty, and not much hope for the school.

Another decade would pass before Jefferson College had a physical presence. The tiny town of Washington had won out over Natchez as the school's site, and it was there that Levi Weeks built the three-and-a-half-story east wing around 1820. Weeks was renowned in the Natchez area for his work on Monmouth, Auburn, the Forest, and Gloucester, and his design for Jefferson College reflected his mastery of the Federal style. The simple lines, strict symmetry, dormer windows, and hipped roof provided an aura of respectability for an institution that desperately needed it to survive.

Less than two years after the first students moved into the new building, Jefferson College closed its doors, the victim of a financial panic and enrollment decline. Fewer and fewer families could afford $22 for a term's tuition and $140 for room and board. The course offerings hardly justified such expenses, and even Governor Poindexter sniffed that the school was merely "an empty dome with pensioned preceptors."[7]

The college struggled along through the antebellum years, frequently suspending operations and usually serving only as a high school–level academy. It did attract such future statesmen and writers as Jefferson Davis, J. F. H. Claiborne and B. L. C. Wailes, in part because the alternatives were scarce and unsatisfactory. Students were exposed to classical studies, mathematics, history, philosophy, and New Testament, with an increasing military emphasis appearing in the years leading up to the Civil War. In 1838, a west wing identical to Levi Weeks's original structure

---

Page 15: Elegant Federal detailing at Jefferson College has been preserved by the Mississippi Department of Archives and History. •

Left: Chartered as Mississippi's first school in 1802, Jefferson College would not have a physical presence for nearly twenty years.

Right: An 1838 west wing mirrored the Federal architecture of Levi Weeks's original building.

was completed, and the two were joined with a central pavilion around 1851.

The onset of hostilities in 1861 dealt the struggling college a hard blow, but it managed to remain open until 1863. Federal troops briefly occupied the buildings in the later years of the war, fortunately inflicting no permanent damage. The long-delayed development of a public school system left Jefferson College without a mission, and it gradually evolved into a small military academy of dubious quality.

By the 1960s, Jefferson College had hung on for more than a century and a half, despite legislative inattention, war, and financial reversals. Its doors were finally padlocked for good after the 1963–64 session, and the buildings began to deteriorate. The 1966 legislature authorized the Mississippi Department of Archives and History to take control of the architecturally outstanding buildings, and the site has been under state control ever since. Family reunions on the site bring back descendants of former students, and Civil War reenactments and living history demonstrations re-create a forgotten time on the campus each year.

Jefferson College hosts family reunions, Civil War reenactments, and craft demonstrations.

WOODVILLE BRANCH BANKING HOUSE

In its territorial and early statehood days, Mississippi was a hotbed of political intrigue, factional spats, and economic chicanery. The southwest corner of the region seemed to attract scoundrels like Aaron Burr and James Wilkinson, shady characters running from the authorities or out to make their fortune in this land of few laws. Duels were fought with little or no provocation, and nothing set tempers off like the long-running dispute over banking.

Natchez was Mississippi's premier city in the first decades of the nineteenth century, and it naturally attracted the initial bank. In 1809 the private Bank of Mississippi was set up by local entrepreneurs eager to rake in the cotton money that was beginning to roll out of the fertile region along the Mississippi River. When statehood was gained eight years later, the Bank of Mississippi was rechartered as the Bank of the State of Mississippi, stamping it as the official lending institution in the new state.

With the population growing and moving into neighboring counties and towns, branches of the all-powerful bank were going to be a necessity. The same legislative Act to Establish a Bank in the Mississippi Territory decreed that outlying locations would be set up in the second- and third-largest towns, Port Gibson and Woodville.

Construction on the Woodville Branch Banking House began immediately and was completed within a year. It reflects the Federal style of the early 1820s, being two stories tall with façades stretching thirty-five feet and thirty-eight feet. Stucco over the brick is scored to resemble ashlar masonry. One long interior room fronts three smaller ones in the rear, and a vault is tucked underneath the stairway. It was fashioned by a Natchez blacksmith, but its locks and the building's doors were cast in New York.

Life was simple and straightforward for the Bank of the State of Mississippi's officers when the entire state's population, for all practical purposes, lived along the strip

of river from Woodville to Port Gibson. It grew increasingly complicated as new Indian cession lands opened up, creating competition for many products, including money. The bank's original charter, heavily influenced by political manipulation, prohibited the establishment of any competing banks before 1840. But by 1830, power had shifted toward Vicksburg, Jackson, and central Mississippi. Legislators from newly formed counties pushed through a charter for Planters' Bank, which absorbed the physical and financial assets of the Bank of the State of Mississippi within a year's time.

The Woodville branch was swept up into the Planters' empire along with the rest of the bank's property. In 1837, an economic panic sent thousands of Mississippians fleeing to Texas, leaving behind notes pinned to their doors with the letters "G.T.T." (Gone To Texas). Planters' Bank collapsed and disappeared. The Woodville building was boarded up and then sold to private investors in 1843.

For the next seventy years, the old bank building served one business after another, buoyed by its prominent location behind the Wilkinson County Courthouse. In 1915, the Woodmen of the World group bought it, converting the upstairs rooms into meeting space and renting the ground floor to barber Joe Plitt. With the Woodville Library occupying the rear rooms, it became a popular informal hangout for generations of townspeople.

Over the years, the physical condition of the branch bank had deteriorated, and it was empty and crumbling when the Woodville Civic Club bought it in 1976, recognizing the worth of its rare Federal architecture. That group stabilized it and has converted it to use as the Wilkinson County Museum of African American History.

Woodville Branch Banking House has served as a financial institution, library, barbershop, and African American cultural museum.

Bowling Green

Wilkinson County, just south of Natchez, is sprinkled with dozens of grand antebellum homes, some dating back to the territorial period before Mississippi's 1817 statehood. They reflect the early prosperity and prominence of Woodville, Fort Adams, and Pinckneyville, frontier towns which were largely forgotten as the state's population and power shifted away from Natchez. The woods and gullies reclaimed many of the old plantations of the region, leaving the houses so far off the beaten path that only a native or an expert guide can locate them.

Many more have been lost to fire and declining fortunes, including three marked by ghostly remnants. The Grove is the most dramatic, with five of its six original Corinthian columns lined up like sentinels deep in the dark forests southeast of Woodville. An 1899 fire consumed all but the brick columns, iron capitals, and shards of the slate roof. West of town, a ruined column is all that remains of Alexander Ventress's LaGrange, also lost to fire a century ago.

Edmund McGehee's 1825 mansion was destroyed by marauding Kansas soldiers, who left only the crumbling columns.

The loss of the Grove and LaGrange were tragic but accidental. Bowling Green, on the other hand, was senselessly destroyed, a victim of war and out-of-control soldiers. It had been built in 1825 by Edmund McGehee, a Georgia native who had made his fortune in railroads, banking, and farming. His Federal-style house, located in the midst of his four-thousand-acre cotton plantation, reportedly rivaled the best of Natchez.

Unlike most of his contemporaries, who were satisfied with growing cotton, shipping it off to New Orleans or Memphis, and accepting a check from their broker, McGehee was intrigued by the fortunes piling up on the manufacturing end of the business. He traveled to Lowell, Massachusetts, to study mill design and returned with plans to duplicate the cloth production facilities in southwest Mississippi. Thomas Weldon of Natchez oversaw construction of the factory just across the road from Bowling Green. Skilled workers were brought in from Alabama, but McGehee soon replaced them with his own slaves. At its peak production, just before the Civil War, McGehee Mills was running four thousand spindles and eighty looms. Close by the factory were three two-story dormitories for the employees.

McGehee was not blind to the evils inherent in the slave system, even though his life was undoubtedly made easier by his nearly five hundred servants and laborers. He was an early participant in the Mississippi Colonization Society, along with Stephen Duncan of Natchez, Isaac Ross of Port Gibson, and many other rich planters. It is unknown whether any of his slaves were freed or repatriated to the society's colony in Liberia.

That enlightened attitude did nothing to save Bowling Green when war crept into Wilkinson County. Natchez had surrendered with arrival of the first Union gunboats beneath its bluffs, and Union troops were barely challenged as they roamed through the area in 1864. It was sheerly by chance that a wandering band of Kansas soldiers stumbled across the factory, which was still turning out gray cloth for the dying Confederate cause. The bored troops set fire to the mill buildings and then stormed across the road to the plantation house. Years later, novelist Stark Young, a cousin of the McGehee family, fictionalized the family legend in *So Red the Rose*:

> The cotton ginhouse across the pasture from the house had been set afire and was burning . . . The house was going to be burnt in twenty minutes . . . They could save what they could . . . The destruction had already begun. The table in the dining room, which had been laid for breakfast, was overturned and smashed for kindling a fire in the middle of the floor. The china closet was crashed up . . . axes smashing over the house, splitting up banisters and furniture for the fire. The pictures on the wall were being slashed or cut down . . . soldiers were pouring turpentine over the

library and a sheet of flame spread there . . . Not long after, flames poured from windows, and down the long hall a torrent of smoke and flame rushed out through the door. Timbers crashed and then the roof fell in. The columns of the front portico remained standing.[8]

Mary McGehee, one of Edmund McGehee's direct descendants, authenticated the fictional tale woven by Stark Young. She recalled older family members telling of the grand piano being dragged from the burning house and the decision to leave the four brick columns standing as a tribute. Colonel McGehee built a new, more modern house above the basement of the destroyed mansion. It was a much simpler frame structure, as most of his fortune had been lost with the destruction of the mill. The family rarely ventured into the basement rooms, shunning them as reminders of their tragic loss.

In 1941, the "new" Bowling Green burned. Once again, the charmed piano was the only salvageable object. This time, the family did not rebuild on the site, but moved into Woodville. The four old columns of the first Bowling Green, their stucco now flaking away and the bricks softening into clay, were left behind. Vines slowly curled up the shafts. At some point, vandals or brick poachers dismantled one column and made away with its bricks.

For several years, when Woodville had an active pilgrimage season, a reenactment entitled "The Burning of Bowling Green" was a highlight of the spring event. Spectators would line up their lawn chairs to sit in the twilight and watch blue soldiers once again storm through with torches and axes, setting fire to an imagined mansion. The tradition was short-lived, and the three remaining columns of Bowling Green now stand quietly in high grass, sad reminders of a great house lost to the savagery of war.

THE HILL

ON THE SOUTHERN FRINGE of Port Gibson, all but invisible from the road, sits an imposing Federal-style mansion known as the Hill. Its once-terraced lawns have vanished beneath the kudzu and creepers, but the house retains the atmosphere that sheltered two of the most memorable characters in Mississippi history.

Peter Van Dorn was a native of New Jersey, born into a prominent Dutch family in the years following the American Revolution. He graduated from Princeton University and set out for the old Southwest territory, eventually turning up in Natchez around 1790. Within a few years, he had made his way up the Mississippi River to Bayou Pierre, joining other early residents of the town that would grow into Port Gibson.

Van Dorn exhibited a political bent, serving as a clerk to Mississippi's territorial superior court and winning election to the legislature. But it was his talent in mapmaking that would carve his place in state history. After a scouting party recommended the site at LeFleur's Bluff for the new capital city, the assembly turned to Van Dorn to lay out a plat of the proposed town. He adapted a plan developed by Thomas Jefferson, sketching out a geometric grid with broad avenues, plentiful parks, and a sweeping Capitol Green high above the Pearl River. He labeled the primary streets Capitol, Congress, State, and President. The symmetry and graceful lines of his creation can still be seen in downtown Jackson, almost two centuries after he mapped it out. The map itself is in the collection of the Mississippi Department of Archives and History.

Following his successful ventures in Jackson, Van Dorn returned to Port Gibson, by now a thriving community with lovely houses built on cotton money. He bought property from the town's founder, Samuel Gibson, just south of the city limits. The site encompassed a large, steep hill. At its apex, his workers built a red brick Federal townhouse, incorporating a formal portico with a fan-lighted entrance door. Tall windows with louvres flanked the portico. Inside, the house included a wide central hall with turned stair and three huge, high-ceilinged rooms on each level.

The landscape surrounding the Hill was as eye-catching as the home itself. Multiple terraces stairstepped down to the main road, and carriage lanes curved up to the house around abundant plantings. From the top of the hill, all of Port Gibson could be seen, laid out like a child's playset.

Peter Van Dorn and his wife, Sophie Donelson Caffery, niece of Rachel Robards Jackson, raised several children at the Hill. The oldest son, Earl, was sent to a Baltimore boarding school after his mother's death, some-time around 1829. He later petitioned his great-uncle by marriage, President Andrew Jackson, for an appointment to West Point.

Succeeding in that appointment and excelling at military training, young Van Dorn was commissioned a lieutenant in the Seventh Infantry in 1842. His exploits in the

The Hill was home to the designer of downtown Jackson, Peter Van Dorn, and a legendary Civil War general, Earl Van Dorn.

Mexican War earned him a promotion to captain and then to major. Further heroics in the Indian wars cemented his reputation as a fearless and often foolhardy soldier.

In 1861, Major Van Dorn resigned his U.S. Army commission. He had kept the family home in Port Gibson throughout his military career, and he quickly declared his loyalty to Mississippi when secession came. Four brigadier generals were appointed by the Mississippi Division of the Confederate Army, and Van Dorn was a logical choice for one of the positions.

His years of battle experience paid off. As commander of the Army of the West, Van Dorn captured the steamship *Star of the West* at Galveston. Ironically, this same boat would wind up back in Mississippi and play a crucial role in blocking General Ulysses Grant's march toward Vicksburg. Van Dorn also humiliated Grant at Holly Springs, where Confederate troops routed sleeping Union forces in a lightning predawn raid that enraged the Federal commander.

The Holly Springs battle was one of Van Dorn's signature forays, demonstrating a daring and somewhat reckless streak that would lead to his downfall. In early 1863, while commanding troops near Spring Hill, Tennessee, Van Dorn became romantically involved with a local doctor's wife. When the physician caught the pair in a compromising situation, he shot and killed Van Dorn. The general's body was brought back to Port Gibson, where he was buried next to his father.

The Hill passed out of the Van Dorn family during the Civil War. For at least ten years, it served as the Presbyterian manse. By the 1930s, its sculpted terraces having long ago disappeared and the carriageways caved in, it was carved into apartments. The State of Mississippi purchased the drastically deteriorated structure in the 1970s to prevent its demolition, and it has been restored and enlarged by architect Doug Lum.

THE
WILKINSON COUNTY
MUSEUM

WEST FELICIANA RAILROAD AND BANKING HOUSE

IN ITS FIRST DECADES, the young state of Mississippi depended on a vast network of waterways and proximity to its namesake river for its vitality. Most of the economy was tied to cotton, and cotton only brought in money if it could be transported from the fields of southwest Mississippi to eager buyers in New Orleans or Memphis. It was a memorable day in Natchez when the first steamboat chugged up to its wharves in 1812, heralding faster transportation and communication. But an even more significant industrial development was just over the horizon. Railroads would open up all of America to development and tie Mississippians more closely to each other and to markets for their agricultural output.

Railroad building was a capital-intensive venture, and innumerable schemes were floated from the late 1820s to the 1840s. Most never progressed beyond words on paper, and

by 1840 the state claimed only eighty-three miles of rails. One of the most well-planned and financed groups was the West Feliciana Railroad, a joint undertaking between entrepreneurial planters and businessmen in Wilkinson County, Mississippi, and West Feliciana Parish, Louisiana. The twenty-nine-mile stretch of rails from Woodville to St. Francisville was recognized as the first interstate line in the South, and its original headquarters still stands as a reminder of that accomplishment.

The Louisiana and Mississippi legislatures passed twin bills establishing the West Feliciana Railroad Company in their 1831 sessions. As was the custom of the day, the resulting corporation would also serve as a bank, and Mississippi granted it full banking privileges two years later. Another three years would pass before actual construction of the line began, and it was predictably plagued with delays and labor disputes. Irish immigrants, infuriated by a contractor's theft of their wages, sued the company for the astronomical sum of $350,000. An unsympathetic judge awarded

---

This Greek Revival structure on the Woodville square housed the offices of the West Feliciana Railroad, the South's first interstate line.

them a grand total of 6½ cents, hardly an incentive for new workers to sign on.

While the railroad slowly snaked from Woodville to St. Francisville, construction of the administration building progressed more quickly. Located at the southeast corner of the courthouse square in downtown Woodville, it was an imposing two-story Greek Revival structure with thick Tuscan columns rising to a simple entablature and hipped roof. The second floor was fronted by an iron-balustraded gallery. Inside, fourteen-foot ceilings, built-in vaults, and an elliptical stair reflected the anticipated prosperity of the corporation.

Fortunately for architectural posterity, the headquarters was finished before the cost of the railroad construction soared from an estimated ten thousand dollars per mile to twenty-five thousand dollars per mile. The initial eight miles were completed by 1836, but it would be another eight years before the first engine lumbered into Woodville, to be greeted by the entire town and much fanfare.

For almost twenty years, the West Feliciana line carried cotton and other produce to the Mississippi River landing at St. Francisville. Passenger cars allowed families to travel between plantations in style. When the Civil War began, the company's directors eagerly offered complimentary service to military outfits and war suppliers. Paper notes, ranging in value from ten cents to twenty dollars, were issued.

By war's end, those notes would serve as the only currency many residents could claim. The railroads cars and tracks were in ruins, and the last remaining engine, Escape, was dismantled for its copper and iron. Southwest Mississippi was a ravaged land, and the once-proud railroad was just a mirror of the wholesale devastation, "[i]ts right-of-way a mass of wood and brambles, its bridges and ties rotting away and its rails but 'two streaks of rust.'"[9]

The railroad lay unused and corroding for more than a decade. Its fine office building was converted to a boardinghouse, and it seemed to many that the trains would never run again from Woodville to St. Francisville. But as Reconstruction wound down and the postwar economy slowly came back to life, the tracks were repaired and a few trains placed on the line. In 1888, the enterprise was purchased by the Louisville, New Orleans and Texas Railroad. Four years later, it was absorbed into the vast Illinois Central network.

The administration building, its railroad origins only a memory, was converted into a post office. In 1949, the county welfare department moved into the high-ceilinged offices. The Woodville Civic Club bought the deteriorating structure in 1973, devoting countless hours to fund-raising, renovation, and conversion to one of the state's finest local museums.

SHIRLEY HOUSE

EIGHTEEN YEARS AFTER Reverend Newit Vick's family laid out a town on Warren County's Walnut Hills, Nicholas Gray was sailing from his home country of Ireland to America. He somehow made his way south to Mississippi and Vicksburg, where he bought several acres of rolling land from T. H. Goodall. On one of his hills, he built a clapboard house facing west and named it Wexford Lodge, in honor of his Irish home.

It was a classically southern-style house, but not a grand mansion like many of those rising in 1830s Mississippi. Wexford Lodge was a one-and-one-half-story structure with a simple front portico. Inside, a wide center hall separated spacious rooms on either side, but there was no elaborate stair or plaster molding. In 1849, it would be described in a real estate ad as "a most desirable residence in a healthy location, 2½ miles from town. The dwelling is 40 feet by 60 feet, containing nine rooms, seven

large ones and a wide passage. There is on the premises a cistern, a spring of never failing water, stable, hen-house, etc. Attached 14 acres of good rich land, a variety of fruit trees, fine range for cattle, winter and summer."[10]

The advertisement caught the eye of James Shirley, a Dartmouth graduate who had moved from New England to Georgia, to Alabama, and, finally, to Vicksburg. Shirley was fifty-seven years old when he purchased Wexford Lodge in 1851, and he undoubtedly expected to spend a quiet and content old age there. He was surely aware of the sectional tension reverberating from the Compromise of 1850 and the rattle of war sabers by Mississippi politicians such as John Quitman, but he could have never anticipated that his "most desirable residence" would one day become the centerpiece of a hellish nightmare of siege and destruction.

The Shirley family imported strong Unionist sentiment with them from New

CLOSED
AREA
DUE TO
CONSTRUCTION

England. Mrs. Shirley was a niece of John Hancock, and one of their sons bore the famous New England name Quincy. When Warren County elected delegates to Mississippi's Secession Convention, James Shirley made no secret of his disgust. His daughter, Alice, recalled the tense days of 1861:

> [My father] had the courage to be true to his convictions, no easy matter when neighbors and friends all flocked to secession and were loud in their denunciation of Union men, calling them traitors. But the little band of Union men had their secret meetings where they talked in low voices and with bated breath exchanging northern news and encouraging each other with hopes that the Federal army must win in spite of all said to the contrary by the boastful south. We still sang our patriotic airs out at the country home, although it was altogether prudent. While there were mutterings of war, my brother Frederick, then a member of a Vicksburg military company, was unwise enough to say that he would rather serve Lincoln twenty years than Jeff Davis two hours. This inflamed the hot-headed young Southerners, and there was loud talk of hanging.[11]

The Shirley servants caught wind of the threats to young Frederick. His trunk was hastily packed, and he

---

Page 31: Scene of carnage and death, the Shirley House was abandoned and nearly lost before the first of a series of restorations.

Left: The Shirley House, caught in the cross fires of the Battle of Vicksburg, is the only antebellum structure in the Vicksburg National Military Park.

was smuggled north to Indiana in the predawn hours. He would not see his family again until after the Civil War.

Alice was sent east to Clinton to attend Central Female Institute. She was boarding with family members there in 1863, as Grant's army plodded toward Vicksburg. When his troops landed at Bruinsburg and fought their way through Port Gibson and Raymond, her alarmed father set out to retrieve her and carry her home to Vicksburg, never realizing that their home was going to be the most dangerous possible site for his family. Alice recounted the scene in Clinton:

> Wednesday morning [May 13] was all excitement. "The Yankees are coming, the Yankees are coming!" The news spread terror to all hearts save a few who secretly rejoiced; two of the few were father and myself. He was so happy that he forgot to think of ourselves or how we were to get home. The people of the village were hurrying hither and yon, the women hysterical, many hiding their jewels and their money. Father and I sat quietly on the long piazza awaiting the coming of the strangers. Along in the afternoon, the first of the blue coats appeared, and oddly enough, came straight to our house, and alighting, walked in and, of course, were given a warm welcome by my father . . . [F]ather spoke of music and invited them into the parlor, where there was a piano, and I played northern and southern patriotic airs, much to their delight . . . Some of them said it had been months since they had spoken to a white lady. I must not forget to mention the other occupants of the parlor; two sacks of live chickens and two turkeys tied behind the

sofa . . . The sound of the piano roused the fowls from their dreams; the chickens squirmed and peeped, the turkeys flapped their wings and used their voices. The officers smiled and looked at each other and then we all laughed.[12]

The light mood was fleeting. While the Shirleys entertained the officers in the family home, the Clinton depot was being torched and the outlying railroad tracks demolished. Line after line of blue troops marched through Clinton, heading west toward Vicksburg. James and Alice Shirley watched them pass: "As my father looked at them I saw the light of a great joy in his eyes; they had come at last, the soldiers of the Union, who carried the old flag so dear to him. He knew their coming meant destruction to his home, to all he owned, for the rear of Vicksburg was their destination, but that was so little compared to the great end. He was willing to lose all . . . that the Union 'must and shall be preserved.'"[13]

Alice's recollections half a century later may have credited her father with more forbearance than he actually possessed. He had no way of knowing that one of the fiercest battles of the nation's bloodiest war was approaching Wexford Lodge and all he cherished. He was determined to make it back to Vicksburg, but the army had obliterated the only rail line between Clinton and home. Sixty-nine-year-old James Shirley headed west on foot, leaving a petulant Alice behind in Clinton.

It would take him several hard days to walk the forty miles, days in which siege lines were laid down and fusillades of bullets and shells began to pound his house. Mrs. Shirley, just as stubborn as her husband, refused to

be evacuated. She and sixteen-year-old Quincy huddled in the house with terrified servants for three long days. All the neighboring houses had already been burned by Confederate troops to prevent their use by Federal forces. A Confederate soldier sent to torch the Shirley house was struck by a stray bullet and crept underneath the porch to die. Still, Mrs. Shirley would not be budged. "My mother and the old home were greeted with a shower of bullets and shell from the advancing [Union] army. One shot passed her as she stood in an open doorway. A piece of shell struck the top of a chimney and tore it away, and passing into an upper room, shattered a bedstead. She thought rapidly; the thing to be done was to hang out a flag of truce, and quickly she secured a sheet to a broom handle, and sending it by our carriage driver to the upper front porch where it might be seen from a distance, it was soon waving a truce to the bullets. The first officers rushed in half expecting to find Confederates hidden away ready to betray them, and were not easily persuaded to believe that we were Union people, and my mother had some talking to do."[14]

The discovery of Alice's pro-Union diary convinced the officers that the Shirleys were truly Union stalwarts. Mrs. Shirley and Quincy were moved into a hastily dug cave with a trunk, a rocking chair, and a blanket rigged up as a makeshift door. When James finally trudged in and found them there a few days later, he packed up the whole clan and moved them beyond the siege lines, first to a plantation house and then to a slave cabin. From there, they listened to weeks of battle and siege, wondering about the fate of their home. James lived long enough to exult at the July 4 Confederate surrender, but a month later he was dead.

Alice, her mother, and her brother returned to find

the Shirley house uninhabitable. In the chaos of postsiege Vicksburg, Alice met and married Chaplain John Eaton, charged with the freedmen settlement in the area. They took Mrs. Shirley with them to Ohio, where they would make their home in more stable circumstances.

The Shirley house sagged into a haunted, blood-stained shell, used briefly as a smallpox hospital and then forgotten. Pleas from Mrs. Shirley for compensation from the federal government were blocked by the Radical Republican–dominated Congress with a new law that forbade repairing houses in rebellious states. It apparently made no difference that the entire Shirley family had risked life and limb for the Union.

As if adding insult to injury, the house was again the scene of horror and death in 1874. Simmering racial tensions after almost a decade of Reconstruction burst into open riots in Vicksburg, and blacks seeking shelter in the skeletal remains of the Shirley house were hunted down and murdered. Vicksburg turned its back on this sad, cursed house, and it collapsed into near-ruin.

Plans to reclaim the battlefield site for a national park surfaced in the 1890s. Alice Shirley Eaton still held title to the old homeplace and its surrounding land, and she was indignant when the National Park Association offered her twenty dollars an acre for the property. "My father died soon after the siege, as much a sacrifice for his country as any soldier who fell in battle . . . my mother, left to depend on me in her last years, went down to her grave mourning the treatment she had received from the Government . . . while I am deeply interested in the Park & would not ask an unreasonable price, as some are doing, I think we have made sacrifice enough."[15]

Alice finally accepted twenty-five dollars per acre for the land and what remained of the house, with the request that "I would like to bury by the old house, my father and mother, whom the war drove from it."[16] The request was granted, the remains were reinterred, and work began on restoration of the house. Alice Shirley Eaton, after more than thirty years, returned to Vicksburg for a tour with the park superintendent. Photos from that time show the once-again handsome house with the brand-new Illinois Monument looming behind it.

During the Great Depression, the Shirley House was again remodeled to serve as the superintendent's home, and it even served briefly as park headquarters. Since that time, it has undergone two major restorations.

OLD CAPITOL

WHEN LEFLEUR'S BLUFF was chosen as the site for Mississippi's new capital city in 1822, it was nothing more than a mosquito-ridden, swampy collection of shanties perched above a bend in the Pearl River. Peter Van Dorn surveyed the surrounding acreage and drew up an inspired vision for Jackson, with broad avenues intersecting at right angles and generous blocks set aside for parks and public buildings.

The largest green was designated for the proposed statehouse, to be built where State and Capitol streets would intersect. It was an ambitious plan for a growing young state's premier city, but it very nearly never happened. Jackson was slow to leave the starting gate, and after ten years, it had attracted almost no permanent residents. Legislators and the governor would scramble to find whatever marginal

Mississippi's Old Capitol has withstood war, neglect, and the winds of Hurricane Katrina over the past 170 years.

accommodations might be available when they were called to meet at the small brick statehouse at the corner of Capitol and President streets. Finding Jackson mainly populated by vermin and snakes and disagreeable to the eye and the nose, they took care of political business and quickly decamped to their homes throughout the state.

By 1832, with the addition of Indian cession lands, north and central Mississippi were rapidly adding new settlers. A new constitution was going to be needed, expanding and complicating duties for both the executive and legislative branches of state government. A more permanent (and impressive) statehouse was necessary, and Van Dorn's Capitol Green awaited its construction. But sentiment throughout the state had turned against Jackson, and the legislature wrote into the new constitution a provision that gave the city exactly eighteen years to prove itself. If it was still provincial and uninviting in 1850, the entire state government would move to a more desirable location.

Jackson had a few friends in the legislature, and they pushed through an appropriation for ninety-five thousand dollars to construct a capitol building on the green. Realizing that more bricks and stone might turn the tide for their city, they also authorized funds for three other essential structures: a governor's residence, state prison, and insane asylum. Their logic was that once the political power, the criminal element, and the mentally ill were housed in Jackson, its future would be secure. It was a logical plan, but was almost derailed by the ineptitude of the man chosen to implement it.

Trained architects were a scarce commodity in antebellum Mississippi. Most of the fine houses of Natchez, Columbus, and Vicksburg were designed and built by frontier carpenters working out of design books. But an ambitious project like the capitol was going to require the very

best talent available, and Governor Abram Scott began the search for a likely candidate. After Scott's death, his successor, Charles Lynch, gave the job to John Lawrence of Tennessee. Governor Lynch was apparently unfazed by Lawrence's application, which misspelled "architect" and was riddled with discrepancies and mistakes. With a contract in hand, Lawrence arrived in Jackson in October 1833, bearing grandiose visions of a massive Gothic Revival statehouse which would rise from the Capitol Green.

The cornerstone for Lawrence's creation was laid in November 1834. As the walls rose, it was quickly apparent to even the most casual observer that something was amiss. Combined with the inherent challenges of Yazoo clay, Lawrence's lack of architectural skills produced a misshapen mess. A year after the groundbreaking, the foundation and one floor were completed, but it bore no resemblance to what the legislature had envisioned for their proud young state. Lawrence was sent packing and the process began anew.

Governor Hiram Runnels was a better judge of artistic talent and competence than his predecessors. He lured William Nichols, a celebrated craftsman who had served as state architect for North Carolina, Alabama, and Louisiana, to Jackson. Nichols had grown up in the architecturally stunning city of Bath, England, and had helped to define the Greek Revival style in America. By bringing him to Mississippi, Governor Runnels was indirectly responsible for some of the state's finest struc-

With the completion of the proposed Museum of Mississippi History, the Old Capitol will be preserved as one of America's finest Greek Revival statehouses.

tural treasures. Nichols would not only design the Old Capitol, but also the Governor's Mansion, the University of Mississippi's Lyceum, and several legendary buildings which have been lost, such as the original State Penitentiary, the Yazoo County Courthouse, and numerous homes and schools.

Nichols arrived in Jackson late in 1835. He quickly realized that Lawrence's Gothic Revival disaster was irreparable and would have to be brought down. Even the members of the legislature had to agree that it was a huge mistake. A committee declared the work to be "against all architectural proportions of order, and the various compartments so bunglingly arranged, as to exhibit neither skill, convenience, nor comfort." Nothing would suffice except a "total and abrupt abandonment."[17]

Nichols set crews to work tearing down the muddled mass of bricks and mortar. In its place, over the next four years, he would fashion a Greek Revival masterpiece, incorporating elements and details which had worked well for him on previous projects. Three stories of red brick with a massive portico, raised basement, and Ionic columns took shape at the east end of Capitol Street, instantly providing a visual and symbolic center to Jackson. It towered above every other building downtown, and as its walls rose higher and higher, it must have been a vindication for all those who had believed in the future of the capital city.

The interior of the new capitol was as imposing as the exterior. The main entrance, accessed beneath the portico, opened onto twin circular stairs and a soaring rotunda. Wings extending off either side led to ornate house and senate chambers, offices, courtrooms, and the state library. Carved columns, gold filigree, and elaborate door sur-

rounds added elegance to the state's largest and grandest public structure.

The work progressed in fits and starts for several years, subject to financial reverses and the whims of the legislature. By 1838, William Nichols was proudly conducting tours of the nearly finished building. Jackson's *Southern Sun* newspaper reported on one such excursion:

> Captain Nichols . . . politely conducted us through the interior of the new state-house, and explained the manner in which it is to be arranged. The more we see of the building, the more we are pleased. The interior will rival in splendor and utility any state-house in the United States, whilst the exterior presents a beautiful outline of architectural symmetry which reflects the highest honor upon its projectors, as well as upon the people of the state . . . We have heard it said that the edifice is too large and too costly for the state. Not at all. Let it be remembered . . . that this is not an edifice designated for a day. It is to stand for a great length of time. Perhaps in the lapse of time, long after we shall have departed this world, those who occupy our stations in society, may point to the moss covered walls of this same building, and venerate it for its antiquity.[18]

The editors were right. The capitol opened to great fanfare and was a source of statewide pride throughout the pre–Civil War years. But its very prominence and symbolism would place it in peril during that war. When the Ordinance of Secession was read from the balcony in January 1861, wild celebrations erupted along Capitol Street. Two years later, as Union troops marched into

Jackson, much of the city went up in flames, and the capitol narrowly avoided destruction. Soldiers tramped through its empty hallways and ripped curtains apart for souvenirs, but miraculously elected not to destroy the building itself.

Reconstruction found various feuding factions of old Confederates, carpetbaggers, and scalawags fussing over office space and power in the capitol. Repairs were made to correct problems already appearing in the thirty-year-old structure, but over the next few decades it would suffer badly from neglect and poor maintenance. William Nichols's grand design began to sag and creak. Tons of state records, moldering in the third-floor library, caused the ceiling to bend ominously above the second-floor courtroom. Legislators gave the suspicious areas a wide berth and began to grumble that a new capitol building was needed. When the state won a million-dollar lawsuit against railroad companies, they got their wish. The old penitentiary was pulled down and a gleaming New Capitol constructed with the legal fees. Legislators, the governor, and state employees, who had nervously waited for the Old Capitol to collapse around them, hurriedly packed up and moved to the more modern structure. They gladly left behind what they considered a dangerous relic of a bygone day.

For more than a decade, the Old Capitol sat empty and decaying on Capitol Green. Columns snapped, the exterior walls pulled away at the corners, and rain poured into the old legislative chambers and offices with every storm. Only the persistence of Dunbar Rowland, Mississippi's first state archivist, and his wife, Eron, kept the wrecking balls from slamming into the bricks of the abandoned building. They rallied local history buffs and women's organizations to their side, and a thirteen-year battle paid off with conversion of the capitol into a state office building. This transformation gave it another fifty-year lease on life. When developers once again eyed the valuable property at State and Capitol in the 1950s, state archivist Charlotte Capers took up the mantle that her predecessor had carried and, once again, renovation bought time for the new state historical museum.

As the writers had predicted in the 1830s, this was a building intended to stand for a long period, even if it was to serve in ways never intended by William Nichols. Its long service as a repository of the state's museum treasures will end with the construction of a new state historical museum. In the summer of 2005, the old building suffered massive damage from Hurricane Katrina's winds, but it is being refurbished by yet another dedicated generation of archivists to serve as a reminder of Mississippi's architectural legacy.

Oakland Chapel

THE HISTORY OF EDUCATION in antebellum Mississippi is one of the more dismal chapters in the state's past. For decades, the legislature and governors railed about the need for academic opportunities, but never followed through with a coherent plan or adequate funding. As a result, anything beyond the most rudimentary exposure to reading and writing was reserved for the rich and well connected. Planters with the means to hire private tutors did so; many sent their sons off to other states for further enlightenment. Lower-class whites suffered from inordinate rates of illiteracy, but were still better off than slaves, who were banned by law from education.

Private entrepreneurs took up the cause of academia in many parts of Mississippi. Their various "academies," "institutions," and "colleges" rarely lived up to their exalted billing, and most disappeared within months or years of their founding. Notable exceptions for young women included Holly Springs Female Institute, Corona College, and Hillman College. For boys, there were a handful of legitimate schools such as Jefferson College, Hampstead Academy, and Oakland College.

Oakland came about through the efforts of the Presbyterian Church and its members in southwest Mississippi.

There was not an institution of any kind on which the Presbytery could write its influence. After viewing these facts, a committee was appointed to go into the matter further. After much correspondence over a period of several months, this committee called a meeting of the friends of Education at Bethel Church, January 4, 1830. This meeting was composed of gentlemen from Louisiana and Mississippi. They were in session six days and adopted the following resolution: "Resolved that it is expedient to establish and endow an institution of learning within our bounds, which when completed shall embrace the usual branches of Science and Literature taught in the colleges of

the country, together with a preparatory English and Classical School and a Theological Professorship or Seminary."[19]

The wisest move the Presbyterians made was to lure Dr. Jeremiah Chamberlain down to the tiny town of Lorman. Chamberlain came armed with a Princeton theology degree and years of experience serving as president of Centre College and Louisiana College. He met with the college's first three students in Mrs. Dromgoole's Lorman home in 1830. The young men must have been impressed and spread the word; within weeks, they were joined by seven more boys and within six months by another twenty-two. Wealthy, well-educated benefactors such as Rush Nutt, Smith Daniell, and Isaac Ross poured money into the school, and plans were laid for permanent buildings.

In 1833, Dr. Chamberlain awarded the first degree earned by a Mississippi native in a Mississippi university to James M. Smilie. His tenure would stretch over two decades. Enrollment continued to increase, with each student charged twelve dollars per month for "diet, washing, fuel and shoe blacking."[20]

Dr. Chamberlain oversaw erection of a president's house, dormitories, and the crowning touch of the campus, Oakland Chapel. Construction began on the three-story, temple-form classroom building in the 1840s. It was a remarkably elaborate structure for a small campus in a remote corner of the state. Two principal floors with

Left: Dr. Jeremiah Chamberlain built Oakland College into an academic powerhouse in early Mississippi.

Right: The Oakland College chapel, faithfully restored, is now the centerpiece of the Alcorn State University campus.

large classrooms and offices topped a raised basement. Six unfluted Doric columns supported a full portico. A square tower, decorated with triglyphs and metopes, could be seen for miles across the countryside.

The chapel was a long-term project. It was probably still under construction when N. G. North of Natchez attended a graduation ceremony: "The weather is delightful. The campus is studded with carriages, horses and servants. The fragrant blooms of the poplar, the dogwood and the locust have called together, in this festive grove, the winged inhabitants of a thousand hives; and, with their humming music, they seem to be playing a lullaby to toilsome cares, and inviting the soul to exult with joy in the feast prepared for her. Away, then, with melancholy!"[21]

Melancholy would eventually be the prevailing sentiment at Oakland College, in spite of its encouraging early years. As sectional tensions increased through the 1850s, the faculty was suspected of harboring northern sentiments or even, most damnably, abolitionists. When Dr. Chamberlain reprimanded a student who had been promoting dissolution of the Union, tempers flared. An

accuser stalked him to his home on campus, lashed him with a buggy whip, and then stabbed him to death.

The glory days of Oakland College died with Jeremiah Chamberlain. In his twenty-year tenure, the school had served more than a thousand students and included among its alumni twenty-one ministers, thirty-nine attorneys, and nineteen physicians. Succeeding presidents struggled with enrollment and monetary challenges. The onset of the Civil War was the last blow. "The college continued until that irrepressible conflict between the States commenced when faculty, students and directors put aside their books for a diversion with rifles and bayonets. At the close of the War, the faculty was gone, most of them killed, the directory was apparently disorganized by death, the property of the college badly abused by the soldiers, who used it as quarters for several months, and the general destruction of property by those engaged in the conflict had sadly diminished the revenue of the college; hence there was not much effort made to reopen the college."[22]

Attempts to revive Oakland College following the war were a dismal failure. The grand chapel, president's home, and dormitories were empty and deteriorating when an unlikely offer came along. Mississippi's Reconstruction government was pushing not only public education for all children but also higher education for freed slaves. Several black colleges were developing under the auspices of northern churches, including Tougaloo College, Shaw University (later Rust College), and Natchez College. When the Presbyterian Church offered to sell the entire Oakland campus to the state, the legislature approved $21,303.28 to complete the deal. Alcorn Agricultural and Mechanical College opened in 1871, headed by Hiram R. Revels, the first black senator elected from Mississippi. He greeted 170 students and 8 professors in the first term, and his school would grow into Alcorn State University.

As the Alcorn campus has grown, the old Oakland Chapel has remained its visual and spiritual center. In 1888, Beaulah Turner Robinson walked across its stage to receive her degree, becoming the first black woman in America to graduate from a state-sponsored university. Two years later, the fire-blackened steps and balustrades from the doomed plantation house Windsor were hauled to Lorman and riveted onto the front of the chapel, where they still stand.

A 1958 tornado heavily damaged Jeremiah Chamberlain's chapel. Major repairs and renovations were undertaken at that time, preserving the building for another century of students. In a small cemetery just west of the campus, Dr. Chamberlain's grave is marked by a shattered shaft, memorializing him as "the beloved father of Oakland College." His school has vanished, but the legacy of educational opportunity he carved out in this corner of Mississippi has been expanded beyond his wildest dreams.

The wrought-iron stair from Windsor, one of the few elements to survive an 1890 fire, was installed on the front facade of Oakland Chapel.

GOVERNOR'S MANSION

TEN YEARS AFTER ITS FOUNDING as Mississippi's planned capital city, Jackson could claim only twelve permanent families. Not one of the state's governors had chosen to live there, and gubernatorial power was so limited that those gentlemen would slip into town, take care of necessary business, and quickly scuttle back home. The charms of Columbia, Natchez, or Biloxi far outweighed the miasmic squalor of 1820s Jackson.

When the legislature gave the struggling town an eighteen-year reprieve, written into the 1832 Constitution, local supporters began to lobby for a permanent statehouse, governor's residence, penitentiary, and insane asylum. Ten thousand dollars was designated for a "suitable house" to serve the chief executive, and newly hired state architect William Nichols was awarded the job of designing and building it.

Nichols spent his first few years in Jackson working on the statehouse. When he finally laid the cornerstone for the Governor's Mansion, he had spent years drafting a house that would equal or surpass any claimed by other states. In keeping with the popular Greek Revival style, the mansion would be a 72' x 53' brick rectangle with a stunning circular portico. Four Corinthian columns and capitals were carved by master craftsman Ezra Williams. The portico would open into an octagonal vestibule. Flanking that formal space were a 50' x 24' drawing room and dining room. A grand stair led up to four bedrooms, and a hidden service stair gave access to the basement's quarters.

The legislature's original appropriation quickly ran dry. Construction was halted within a year of its onset, and Nichols moved on to other projects until the financial picture improved. Zinc strips lining the incomplete roof of the house peeled away, allowing water to pour into the attic and down the interior walls. The resulting plaster damage would plague gubernatorial families and curators for more than a century.

When construction finally resumed in 1841, it was a race against time to prepare the home for incoming

Governor Tilghman Tucker. After years of delays and budget overruns that had quadrupled the original estimates, the unfurnished mansion was handed over to the new state leader in February 1842. Governor Tucker found six empty, echoing rooms, bare of a single stick of furniture. Wagons were dispatched to Lowndes County, and the first furnishings of the brand-new mansion were all Tucker property.

The Governor's Mansion was an architectural gem, but its grounds were sadly neglected. An 1840s observer sniffed that they looked much like his weedy cow pasture. Governor Albert Gallatin Brown's wife set out along Capitol Street, planting cedars all the way to the capitol building, and beautified the mansion grounds with rosebushes and honeysuckle vines.

For its first two decades, the Governor's Mansion witnessed a mostly forgettable procession of politicians going through its doors, punctuated by the occasional true statesman or zealot. Mexican War hero John A. Quitman livened up the hallways with his fire-breathing secessionist rhetoric. John J. Pettus was in residence when crowds roared down Capitol Street in January 1861, wildly celebrating Mississippi's secession from the Union. That fateful decision would lead the mansion dangerously close to oblivion, as the Civil War swept right up to its doorstep and into its rooms.

Spring of 1863 found Governor Pettus, General John C. Pemberton, and General Joseph E. Johnston huddling in the mansion as Union forces pushed towards Vicksburg. By May, the governor had advised state officials to prepare for evacuation at a moment's notice. When General Johnston rode into Jackson on May 13, he found an eerie ghost town. The mansion was deserted; the governor, his family, and staff had hastily packed their personal belongings and the state papers and fled to east Mississippi. Johnston declared the city indefensible and headed west for Vicksburg. Within twenty-four hours, Jackson was overrun with Union soldiers. Generals Grant and Sherman personally delineated which buildings were to be burned, but they mercifully excluded the governor's house from their list.

When Governor Pettus crept back into town in late May, he found a devastated city. His home had been turned into a hospital, and it is unknown whether he even stopped by there. He was gone by the time Union troops returned to Jackson for another round of destruction. General Sherman set up his occupation headquarters in the abandoned mansion, and was surrounded by his troops' tents on Mrs. Brown's manicured lawns.

After Sherman and his troops moved on, the Governor's Mansion sat empty for two years. Governor Pettus and his successor, Charles Clark, did not dare return to the capital city or their official residence. The nomadic state government roamed from Enterprise to Meridian, from Macon to Columbus, as soldiers repeatedly occupied Jackson. When the war at last ended, Governor Clark ordered the scattered remnants of the government to return to Jackson. The legislature met one time and fled after rumors of their impending arrest circulated through the capitol. On May 22, 1865, the governor signed over all state property, including the Governor's Mansion, to the federal commissioner. The war was over, but the mansion grounds would be a political battleground for another decade.

William Nichols's masterpiece has housed Mississippi's governors on Capitol Street since 1842.

The next few years were ones of turmoil and confusion as Mississippi struggled toward repatriation as a state. Elected officials vied with occupation forces for control of the state's power and buildings. Benjamin G. Humphreys won election as governor in 1865; after his inauguration, he found the mansion stripped of furniture but otherwise inhabitable. He moved his family into the dusty rooms and set about trying to get Mississippi back on its feet. Unfortunately, the recalcitrant legislature refused to ratify the Thirteenth and Fourteenth Amendments to the Constitution and enacted the notorious Black Codes. Radical Republicans in Congress took this as too much of a challenge to tolerate and slapped military rule onto Mississippi.

Adelbert Ames was sent south as Mississippi's provisional governor. While Congress and the military may have recognized him as the state's chief executive, Benjamin Humphreys did not. Ames was at a loss; he had nowhere to live in the wasted city and minimal guidance for dealing with a stubborn but duly elected governor. He sent word to the Humphreys family, asking them to please vacate the mansion. Governor Humphreys, already expelled from his capitol office, was furious. Ames then graciously (in his mind) offered to share the mansion with the Humphreys family. He was met with a stony refusal. On July 13, 1868, he sent a bewildered lieutenant to the mansion with an ultimatum. Mrs. Humphreys wrote to her mother of the ensuing scene: "Monday morning General Ames wrote to the Governor that he wanted the Mansion. This, of course, has changed our plans for the summer . . . Old Veto [Governor Humphreys], of course, refused to surrender the Mansion . . . I am placed in command of the Mansion, with orders to hold it at all hazards . . . [W]e can hold the enemy in check, whenever he makes the attack, until the Governor can come to our support. I think this step brings affairs to a climax."[23]

A climax was indeed imminent. "Well, Monday morning came and with it the Yankee raid upon the Mansion . . . We packed up everything that belonged to us and were ready for the attack, which was made about 12 o'clock. Lieutenant Bach, commanding a file of six soldiers, rode up to the gate. The Lieutenant dismounted and came in. Gov. Humphreys met him at the front door, the Lieutenant said 'good morning' and offered his hand, which was not received . . . [H]e had been sent by Col. Biddle to take possession of part of the mansion. Gov. said he refused to give it up . . . Mr. Humphreys asked him if he would carry out the order to put him out by force? He said he would."[24]

The entire Humphreys family was marched out across the portico between bayoneted ranks of soldiers. Adelbert Ames moved into the mansion, and the rumors of his misconduct and ill manners started immediately, fanned by the incensed Mrs. Humphreys. "He has had a billiard table put in one of the parlors, after dark he and his friends go and play billiards . . . I have heard he spends most of his time in the billiard room, and was *drunk* last Saturday . . . We never hear him spoken of but with contempt."[25]

Whatever the state of his sobriety, Ames lived in the mansion from 1868 to 1870 and again from his election in 1875 to the time of his threatened impeachment in 1876. He described his years there as prisonlike, with his children cautioned never to venture beyond the fence.

Mississippi was solidly under local control again by the latter decades of the nineteenth century, and the

Governor's Mansion was the scene of much entertaining and gaiety but little or no maintenance. Telephones were installed in 1882; running water and electricity were added six years later. But the land that the mansion sat on was becoming increasingly valuable, particularly in the booming years of the early 1900s. Developers eyed the land for profit and leaned on the governors and legislators to tear down the decrepit old mansion.

Governor after governor begged the legislature for funds to shore up the house until other arrangements could be made. Each was ignored. James K. Vardaman was horrified at its condition when he moved his family in, branding it a "relic of aristocracy" and affirming his populist roots with the addition of a cow to the grounds. But by the time he made his farewell address to the legislature at the end of his term, he had grown to love the fading mansion. "I am very much opposed to selling this property . . . Besides being a most beautiful piece of architecture, it has a sentimental value which cannot be measured in dollars and cents."[26]

Vardaman's successor wasn't so sure. Edmond Noel literally feared for the safety of his wife and children after he saw the condition of his appointed house. He moved them into the Edwards House at the far end of Capitol Street and told the legislature that the "venerable pile of crumbling brick" he had been given would not do for the Noel family.

His harsh words struck a chord, but not in the legislature. In this age of Confederate veneration, with memorial plaques and stone soldiers popping up on every courthouse square throughout the state, Noel had riled up the most formidable constituency in Mississippi. The matrons of Mississippi rose up in anger and turned wrath toward the men sitting in the New Capitol. Senators and representatives scampered for cover as waves of United Daughters of the Confederacy, Daughters of 1812, the Women's Temperance Union, and even the Old Ladies Home Association descended on them like a bibilical plague.

Predictably, the women won. The thoroughly cowed legislature quickly passed appropriations of thirty thousand dollars for repairs to the mansion and construction of a new two-story family annex. The original iron fence was removed, the grounds were spruced up, and concrete driveways were installed. Exterior stonework was pulled away and replaced with yellow brick. On the interior, the original faulty plaster was taken down and the stair was moved to the center of the main hallway.

The mansion was saved for the moment, but age continued to take its toll, and by the 1970s it was once again deemed unsafe for the governor's family. Under the guidance of First Lady Carroll Waller, a massive restoration was begun, with replacement of the 1908 annex. The stairway was placed back in its original 1841 location, and a high brick fence was erected around the grounds. Since that effort, the mansion has been maintained and modernized, now secure in its position as one of the oldest executive mansions in America.

CLIFTON

THE BUILDING BOOM that engulfed Mississippi during the first half of the nineteenth century largely bypassed the Delta region. Thickly forested with cypress, oak, and cedar trees and blanketed with languid bayous, the northwest corner of the state would not be extensively developed until levees brought the annual spring floods under control. The money and muscle of railroads would arrive after the Civil War, opening the Delta to its peak agricultural years and consequent development.

Because it was so sparsely populated in the prewar years, the Delta has only a handful of antebellum mansions. Several small plantation communities arose around Lake Washington and further north near the Mississippi River, leaving such homes as Belmont, the Burrus House, and Mount Holly. Between those river counties and the loess bluffs fifty miles to the east, such houses were rare and most have not survived. The exception is Clifton,

a mysterious Greek Revival home tucked just beneath the bluffs in Holmes County.

The intriguing oddity of Clifton is its resemblance to Beauvoir, Jefferson Davis's beachside home in Biloxi. Beauvoir was known to have been designed and built by Madison County planter James Brown in the late 1840s. Careful comparison of that house and Clifton reveal striking, almost identical details. Both are Greek Revival raised cottages, with porches on three sides, a central stair leading to the porches, and a centrally placed door with two long windows on either side. Square columns support hipped roofs, and latticework stretches between the columns' supports around the basement level.

While Beauvoir's early history is well documented, Clifton's is murky. The architect and builder are unknown, leading to speculation that Mr. Brown might have been involved, given the proximity of Madison and

Holmes counties. The plantation was definitely owned by William Frisby Stansbury by the 1850s, and he had spent time living on the Gulf Coast. Perhaps he had admired Beauvoir and had his builder copy the design. Evidence to refute that theory evolved from a beam recovered from a rotted gazebo at Clifton, bearing the faint inscription "Dec. 1839." If the house were standing then, it would have predated Beauvoir.

Regardless of its early origins, Clifton was the home-place of a functioning Delta plantation by the mid-1850s. The Stansbury family lost control of it during the Civil War, and it was purchased, sight unseen, by a northern specula-tor, Myron Waters. Waters was a Pennsylvania oilman who recognized the opportunity for buying up distressed prop-erty in the South following the war. He scooped up several sites in Mississippi, undoubtedly hoping for a handsome return on his investment as rebuilding commenced.

Waters's main problem was oversight of his far-flung speculative empire. Fortunately for him, his brother-in-law, Liberty Constantine Abbott, a veteran of the Fifth New York Cavalry, was posted to Corinth, Mississippi, to help with Reconstruction. Abbott subsequently served as a federal district judge, land commissioner, and at other posts, but he yearned to settle in his new state as a gentle-man farmer. When Waters offered him the chance to move to Holmes County and run Clifton, he grabbed it. He left behind war and Reconstruction politics and sank his roots between Tchula and Lexington.

Abbott lived at Clifton until his death in 1897; his wife used life insurance payments to buy the house and planta-tion, totaling 1,280 acres, from her in-laws. Her sister and brother-in-law moved down from Ohio to join her and her daughter, Birdie, a crippled victim of polio. Birdie had recently married a Holmes County native, Peyton Tabb Jones, placing one more barrier between the family and the old stigma of "carpetbagger."

The Abbott and Jones family owned Clifton for sev-eral generations. The upstairs space of the house was con-verted to a classroom, where William Frisby Stansbury's daughter, Claudine, taught school. Other renovations and improvements were made over the years, including a coal-

Previous page left: The old bell at Clifton is one of many surviving details from its days as an active cotton plantation in Holmes County.

Previous page right: Clifton is one of the few extant examples of antebellum architecture in the Mississippi Delta.

Top: The members of Clifton Plantation Hunting Preserve have meticulously maintained and improved the main house and added private cabins for their members.

fired furnace and, finally, in the 1930s, electrical power. Before the Rural Electric Association lines reached Clifton, Birdie had rigged up a battery bank in one of the cistern houses, providing less-than-satisfactory DC power.

Frank Abbott Jones, who grew up at Clifton, recalled a tornado roaring through in 1940. The family was huddled in the cellar with a kerosene lamp. "The sounds of the storm raging about us defy description. The unrelenting wind assailing the front doors sounded truly like the wail of a banshee. This mournful shriek was underscored by the roar of the wind and the sound of the rain which was more like standing under Niagara Falls than in a mere rainstorm. Amid the lightning and thunder of the tempest, we could feel the house tremble, and interspersing all this was the sound of all those regal cedars suddenly cracking as they reluctantly yielded to the storm's fury."

The storm had wreaked havoc on the four long avenues of cedars which had shaded the house since its erection. "The front rooms and the end of the hall took the brunt of the storm; the front doors had blown open during the night, and rain soaked debris—a mixture of limbs, glass and plaster—made passage to the porch difficult. There we could finally view the devastation the sounds of which had so terrified us in the darkness of the cellar the night before. Over 30 giant fallen cedars, some of them two feet in diameter, covered the ground completely in an evergreen sea. The destruction was total, not a one left standing."[27]

Clifton had weathered a direct tornado strike with minimal structural damage. Unfortunately, human effort left some permanent scars. "The next 3 months everyone's attention was focused on clearing the yard of the cedar boughs . . . The trunks and large limbs were split into fence posts; smaller limbs were saved for kindling and firewood; the boughs were hauled away. Finally only the stumps remained . . . it was decided to blast them out with dynamite. Sticks of dynamite were inserted around and underneath the stumps; the caps were attached by wire to the detonator under the front porch. It worked quite well, except no one foresaw the damage to the plaster inside the house. Later hairline cracks appeared and over time lengthened and widened, until ultimately chunks of plaster became dislodged and fell to the floor—much like the effect of a rock chipping the windshield of an automobile."[28]

Despite the storm- and dynamite-inflicted damage, Clifton survived for another forty years as a functioning plantation. In the 1980s, it was sold to Clifton Plantation Hunting Preserve, whose members have meticulously maintained and protected it. Few structural changes have been made, and it has been the site of weddings, reunions, and family gatherings that would have made its unknown builder proud.

JACKSON CITY HALL

JACKSON IS THE CAPITAL CITY that nearly wasn't. Its first years were so wretchedly unappealing that the state government and the few intrepid settlers who had moved in were threatening to pack up and decamp to Vicksburg, Clinton, Port Gibson, anywhere but Jackson. Three existing downtown buildings testify to the determination of a few to salvage Jackson and make it a livable city. The Old Capitol, the Governor's Mansion, and Jackson City Hall are rare reminders of the young city's eventual antebellum opulence.

When Mississippi was awarded statehood in 1817, the site which would become Jackson was nothing more than a brackish backwater on the thinly traveled Pearl River. The state had fourteen formal counties lining the Mississippi River and the Gulf Coast. Congress had laid out the southern border of Tennessee as the new state's northern edge, but the upper two-thirds of the state were occupied by only Choctaws and Chickasaws. It was logical that all government business was conducted in Natchez and nearby Washington.

The Treaty of Doak's Stand, signed in 1820, changed all that. When General Andrew Jackson and Thomas Hinds signed the deal with the Choctaw Indian chiefs, a huge tract of land was suddenly open for development. The entire parcel of 5.5 million acres, which would constitute the western part of the middle third of Mississippi, was originally designated Hinds County. As tracts were sold off and pioneers flocked in, it quickly became evident that a more centrally located capital than Natchez would be necessary.

The 1821 general assembly met in Natchez and effectively turned its back on that venerable city. A yellow fever outbreak chased the assembly to Columbia, but that site never received serious consideration as a permanent seat of government. The assembly chose Thomas Hinds, James

Jackson's city hall was designed by William Gibbons and miraculously survived the destruction of most of the capital city in 1863.

Patton, and William Larrimore to venture into the wilds of central Mississippi and locate a capital site within twenty miles of the state's geographic center.

That exact center was the aforementioned Doak's Stand, in what is now southeastern Madison County. It lacked river access and well-drained land, and the commissioners could not decide on an opportune spot for a capital city. They headed back south and stumbled on the tiny trading post at LeFleur's Bluff, overlooking the Pearl River. Their reports to the assembly were glowing: "LeFleur's Bluff is situated about ten miles south of the Choctaw Agency House, on the west side of the Pearl River . . . and elevated, according to information, about twenty or twenty-five feet above the highest floods . . . About eight hundred yards obliquely from the river, is presented, from an eastern position, a beautiful eminence, continuous with the bluff, agreeably undulating, and of ample extent."[29]

With such enthusiastic recommendations, the assembly gave its approval to the site and hired Peter Van Dorn of Port Gibson to draw up a plat for Jackson. Van Dorn's 1822 map features a Jeffersonian-inspired grid of streets, with now-familiar names such as Congress, State, Capitol, and Pearl, intersecting at right angles to produce squares, greens, and park spaces. One of the largest squares, just west of the Capitol Green, would be the site of the city hall.

What Van Dorn's map did not show were the sluggish swamps generated by the Pearl River, huge mosquitoes, alligators, and snakes. Nor did it show the frequent rains that turned the infant town's dirt paths into muddy, impassable bogs. Legislators, called into session at the small statehouse thrown up at the corner of Capitol

and President streets, would conduct their business and light out again for home. A few decrepit boardinghouses opened, but almost no permanent homes were built during the first decade of Jackson's existence. The future seemed precarious for the new capital city.

The rest of Mississippi was booming. The Treaty of Dancing Rabbit Creek in 1830 threw open the doors to north Mississippi, swelling the population and leading to a constitutional convention in 1832. With so many new people piling in, the state government required expansion and buildings to house services. A large element in the legislature wanted to abandon Jackson; competing factions wrote in a clause giving the city eighteen years of grace. If conditions remained unbearable in 1850, Jackson would give up its status as capital.

Jackson boosters finally coalesced and pushed through appropriations for a new statehouse, a governor's residence, a state penitentiary, and an insane asylum. William Nichols was hired as state architect, and for much of the 1830s and 1840s, Jackson was buzzing with the construction of those four essential structures. By the time the grand new capitol building was dedicated in the late 1830s, Jackson's future was secure.

With its existence no longer in doubt, Jackson now needed its own municipal government and image. Thomas H. Dickson was chosen from the first panel of selectmen to serve as mayor. In May of 1846, a resolution was passed by the governing body to immediately erect a suitable city hall, to be designed and built by William Gibbons. The square of available land west of the capitol was claimed, and construction was under way by June. The original plans called for a two-story building; pressure from the local Masonic chapter led to the addition of a third floor, paid for and dedicated to the Masons' use.

It took barely a year to finish the huge building. In keeping with the style of the day and the tone set by the neighboring capitol and Governor's Mansion, it was designed as a Greek Revival block. Stucco covers brick, and massive Doric columns support a full formal pediment. An odd arrangement of interior floors leads to a confusing illusion; the hall seems to have two stories on its east side and three on its west.

In 1852, the city hall was either rebuilt or enlarged. Contemporary news accounts mention a cornerstone-laying ceremony but are unclear as to the extent of the work done.

When the Civil War swept into Jackson in 1863, city hall was endangered by the wholesale torching of any buildings which General Sherman found threatening. Various sources credit the salvation of the hall to General Grant's Masonic membership or its use as a hospital. Regardless, it was one of the few substantial buildings remaining after Federal occupation. A reporter for *Frank Leslie's Illustrated Newspaper* described the carnage surrounding the site:

> Jackson was first entered by the Federal troops on the 14th of May, 1863. General Grant's army was then moving on Vicksburg. In his official report of the preliminary operations respecting his capture of Vicksburg, he says: "Sherman was left in Jackson to destroy the railroads, bridges, factories, workshops and everything valuable for the support of the army," and this, he added, very truly, "was accomplished in the most effectual manner." Among the buildings destroyed at this time were the State Penitentiary, the factories of Phillips and Green, the Confederate House, the Catholic Church, the railroad depot, and about four squares of the business portion of the city, with several handsome residences in the suburbs. The effect upon the non-combatants, as may be imagined, was appalling. On every side, where once stood splendid stores, warehouses, and magnificent residences, embosomed in tropical shrubbery, naught remained but charred and smoldering ruins.[30]

The survival of the city hall, the capitol, and the Governor's Mansion, all symbols of Confederate pride, was nothing short of miraculous. From within the walls of city hall, Mayor Henry Manship and his staff struggled to rebuild Jackson's government and basic services. The ensuing years saw explosive growth in the city, and the hall changed to accommodate new times and new needs. The domed cupola on the east side was removed in 1874; fifty years later, the old public gas works were torn out on the west side and a formal portico built to match the east façade. At that time, formal gardens were planted, and these, along with the statue of General Andrew Jackson, have come to symbolize downtown Jackson.

A massive renovation of the city hall was undertaken in 1963, stabilizing the aging building with steel and concrete reinforcements.

Little Red Schoolhouse

Hidden in a corner of Jackson's downtown Smith Park, just a stone's throw behind the Governor's Mansion, is a little-noticed marker commemorating the Order of the Eastern Star. It seems an odd spot for such a memorial, but no odder than the sight of an imposing two-story red brick schoolhouse rising above Holmes County cotton fields fifty miles north of the capital city. The two sites are intimately connected through their association with Rob Morris, a Victorian educator and visionary whose innovations continue to have an impact on Masonic rituals today.

Dr. Robert Morris was a Massachusetts native who somehow made his way south to the young town of Oxford, Mississippi, in the early 1840s. Records document his initiation into the Oxford Masonic Lodge in March 1846, and his fellow Masons were impressed enough with his

academic credentials to place him in charge of the Mount Sylvan Academy there.

He wouldn't tarry in Oxford for long. Unknown to Morris, the Masonic Lodges of Holmes County had raised thirty-four hundred dollars to erect a "handsome brick edifice, 60 feet by 30 feet, and two stories high."[31] The Richland Literary Institute's cornerstone was laid in October 1847, and its charter name changed to Eureka Masonic College the following year. The school was one of numerous privately endowed institutes springing up throughout Mississippi, as individuals, churches, and benevolent organizations struggled to address the state's abysmal educational offerings.

Considering the isolation of its site, the college's lone building was quite an accomplishment. Its primary façades face east and west, with the impression of a Federal-style fanlight created in brick over the doorways. The windows are long and rectangular with louvered shutters. Each gable end is pierced by a small chimneytop with no exterior evi-

dence of the shaft. Inside, a stair hall divides the first floor into two large classrooms. Upstairs is a single open room.

Once Eureka Masonic College's single brick building was completed, finding a headmaster was the next order of business. Robert Morris's reputation as an active Mason and the author of several books on Freemasonry caught the attention of the Holmes County society, and he was lured away from Oxford. The nature of the Mount Sylvan Academy facilities is lost to time, but Morris must have been impressed at the sight of what was, undoubtedly, the largest building in rural Holmes County, ready and waiting for his academic talents.

As his teaching career advanced and he delved more deeply into the rituals of the Masonic order, Morris became increasingly dissatisfied with the women's position in the organization. Since the early 1800s, wives of Masons had been endowed with titles such as "Heroines of Jericho" and "Tall Cedars of Lebanon," but they had no real standing in Freemasonry and no hierarchy of their own. Morris found these quasi-degrees to be "rather thin—g[iving] but little satisfaction—barren in matter and inartistic in form, and I was convinced that something better could be made."[32]

Morris brooded over the perceived slights to his female friends and students for several years. A time of convalescence, either from an arthritic condition or an accident, left him in a downtown Jackson home for an extended period in 1850. Freed temporarily from his teaching and

Top right: The Little Red Schoolhouse has served as a Masonic college, Civil War regimental headquarters, and a public school.

Bottom right: The Order of the Eastern Star has restored the Little Red Schoolhouse to its 1850s appearance.

administrative duties, he devoted all his mental energy to the development of a women's Masonic organization. "In the winter of 1850 I was a resident of Jackson, Mississippi. For some time I had contemplated . . . the preparation of a Ritual of Adoptive Masonry . . . About the first week of February, 1850, I was laid up for two weeks with a sharp attack of rheumatism, and it was this period which I gave to the work at hand . . . So my ritual was complete, and after touching and retouching the manuscript, as professional authors love to do, I invited a neighboring Mason and his wife to join with my own, and to them in my own parlor, communicated the Degrees. They were the first recipients."[33]

Morris was consumed with the implementation of his new scheme, and it is unclear whether he ever returned to his leadership position at Eureka Masonic College. The school's offerings never advanced beyond a precollege preparatory level, and in 1861 it ceased operations. The empty building was pressed into service as the regimental headquarters of Company C, Fifteenth Mississippi Infantry, as the volunteers drilled and anticipated their mustering into the Confederate Army. They marched off to fight at Shiloh, Vicksburg, Franklin, and various battles in the Atlantic Coast campaign.

Following the Civil War, the abandoned schoolhouse was deeded to Holmes County, which converted it into one of Mississippi's first public schools for blacks. It would serve in this capacity for almost a century, but it suffered from the state's notorious neglect of "separate but equal" funding. WPA writers of the 1930s found a sad spectacle: "The school is a two-story brick building, with its structural material so deteriorated that it has become necessary to brace the building with iron rods extending its width and fastened to the outside walls with huge iron washers."[34]

Twenty years later, Holmes County had shuttered the building, moving its students to more modern facilities. The school was leased back to the Order of the Eastern Star, which by now had grown into a worldwide society with more than a million members. In memory of their founder, Dr. Morris, they began a long and arduous restoration. Bricked-over windows were reopened, the Federal-style detailing was restored, and the two large classrooms on the first floor were converted into museum and archival spaces. The second floor dormitory room was redesigned as a meeting hall. Fireplaces were unsealed on both floors.

In August 1968, full title to the building, now affectionately known as the Little Red Schoolhouse, was granted to the Eastern Star order. It is maintained as a historic shrine commemorating their group and its founder. Each summer, hundreds of members converge with their families to picnic and celebrate Rob Morris, who carved out a place for them in Freemasonry.

LYCEUM

MISSISSIPPIANS IN THE first decades of their state's existence were mainly concerned with the most elemental needs for survival. Education, culture, and organized religion were often overlooked in the struggle to provide food and shelter and to maintain an economy that ran primarily on cotton money. But many of those who came from New England and the Atlantic Coast states had left behind a tradition of higher education, and they became increasingly adamant about the need for a state university as time went on.

The legislature, even in the territorial period, had made occasional feints at funding a public college. Jefferson College was chartered in 1802 but not operational for almost a decade, and its location in the far southwestern town of Washington made it an impractical choice for a statewide

Completed in 1848, the University of Mississippi Lyceum was extensively restored in the 1990s, with the uncovering of many long-forgotten architectural details.

institution of higher learning. The University of Holly Springs actually received a charter and opened for a few brief months in the 1830s, but an economic downturn doomed it before it could truly be considered the state university.

In 1840, Wilkinson County representative James Alexander Ventress, chairman of the House Committee on Seminary Funds, introduced a bill to "provide for the location of the State University." It was time to stop the drain of Mississippi's young academic talent to neighboring states and points north. A joint legislative committee nominated seven potential sites for the new school: Louisville, Kosciusko, Mississippi City, Brandon, Middleton, Monroe Missionary Station, and Oxford. Multiple votes winnowed the choices down to Monroe, Mississippi City, and Oxford. On January 21, 1841, the lawmakers chose Oxford on a fifty-eight to fifty-seven vote.

The "University of Mississippi" existed in name only. A site had to be selected in Lafayette County, cleared, and readied for multiple buildings. The choice of an architect for the campus was an obvious one. William Nichols had spent the previous decade serving as Mississippi's state architect, and the results of his talents were evident in the statehouse, the Governor's Mansion, and the State Penitentiary. He moved his tools and drafting boards to Oxford and set to work designing a university from scratch.

Nichols submitted plans for two faculty houses, each with twelve rooms suitable for two families. Two dormitories would house seventy-two young men, the projected initial enrollment, and a steward's hall would be the functional element of the array. Centered among these structures would be the crowning achievement of Nichols's long architectural career: a five-bay, three-story Greek Revival academic building, with a pedimented portico supported by colossal Ionic columns. The original drawing featured a raised basement, a style that Nichols had perfected in the Alabama and Mississippi state capitols. The college's board of trustees approved all of his proposals except the Lyceum basement, and Nichols began work on the six seminal structures of the university.

Hundreds of Oxford citizens, including the volunteer fire company, clergymen, Freemasons, and the board of trustees marched from the courthouse square to the cleared building site on July 14, 1846. With much pomp and ceremony, the Lyceum cornerstone was laid—a hollow block containing a Bible, various papers, and coins. For the next two and one-half years, workers clambered over scaffolding, laying the red bricks and smoothing plaster onto the giant columns. When the first students arrived in November 1848, they had to skirt around brick kilns and random scraps of lumber, but the Lyceum was open and ready to go. Four faculty members, including twenty-seven-year-old President George Frederick Holmes, moved into the teachers' quarters. By the following summer, eighty students were on campus and the University of Mississippi was a functioning reality.

John Newton Waddel, one of the school's earliest professors, was present that first term and described William Nichols's central building: "The Lyceum was an imposing structure of the height of three stories, and with a front portico supported by six large and handsome columns. It contained, on the first floor, two rooms, and a large chemical theatre for lectures, and a laboratory running back, of large dimensions. In the second story was, in front, a fine room devoted to a collection of shells and geological and mineral specimens of great value and beauty; and besides this room, were four rooms for lectures and recitation purposes. The third floor was occupied at that time by the library and similar rooms, corresponding to those of the second story."[35]

The university was an immediate success, and the classrooms of the Lyceum were soon filled beyond capacity. A west wing addition increased space by one-third. More structures were being built around campus, including the chapel and Barnard Observatory.

Archival photos of the day show a readily recognizable Lyceum with slouch-hatted students at stiff attention on the front steps. Most of those young men left in 1861, eagerly signing up for the University Greys and other infantry and artillery units around the state. When only a handful of returnees showed up for the fall semester, the college was closed for the duration of what was expected to be a short and triumphant war for the South.

Professor of Latin Alexander Quinche was left with the keys to the buildings, which he probably assumed would simply be shuttered and maintained until the conflict ended. When war swept into northeast Mississippi after battles at Shiloh and Corinth, Quinche found his Lyceum, observatory, and dormitories desperately needed as hospital space. The Confederate forces moved on, Union troops commandeered the campus, and it took all the persuasive powers of Quinche and state geologist Eugene Hilgard to prevent wholesale demolition of the university. General A. J. "Whiskey" Smith was dissuaded from torching the Lyceum, although he showed no such mercy for Oxford itself.

After the Confederate surrender at Appomattox, the university reopened and struggled to provide a degree of normalcy and academic endeavor during Reconstruction. As the decades went by, the original buildings were gradually replaced by more modern counterparts, leaving the Lyceum as the sole representative of William Nichols's design. No serious suggestions were raised to demolish this beloved icon, but it did have to adapt with the times. In 1903, north and south wings were added to the original block, more than doubling the available space while maintaining the Greek Revival symmetry that Nichols had so valued. In 1948, a major renovation was undertaken, updating the Lyceum at its century mark.

Exactly one hundred years after violence had first visited the University of Mississippi, it arrived again with the onset of integration. Federal marshals encircled the Lyceum, facing down an enraged mob determined to block the enrollment of the first black student. Images of the proud old building, hazy through tear gas clouds and surrounded by armed soldiers, were seen around the world. Administrator Hugh Clegg was watching from the chancellor's residence across the Circle. "We all [sat] on the Chancellor's porch, watching the sickening scene from a hundred yards away. Automobiles were afire. We feared the Lyceum Building would be burned."[36] Bullets nicked the columns and interior plaster of the Lyceum, in what Willie Morris described as "an echo of the Civil War's last battle."[37]

The Lyceum survived the insanity of that September, as it had survived Civil War and years of neglect, inevitable in this poorest of states. In the late 1990s, an $11 million renovation gutted the building, with its original elements tagged and stored away. Steel beams were inserted in the exterior walls. Workmen uncovered long-forgotten fireplaces behind the plaster of the formal front reception rooms. Evidence of the south wing's previous function as a gymnasium was also discovered, as were beaded ceilings in the second-floor rooms. The lost cornerstone was retrieved, still holding its treasures from 1848.

The Ole Miss campus has spread and expanded and enveloped the first buildings of that 1848 school, but the Lyceum remains, an emotionally charged link through a century and a half of Mississippi history.

Biloxi Lighthouse

In the aftermath of Hurricane Katrina, as stunned Gulf Coast residents ventured out to find most of their homes, businesses, and towns smashed, one indomitable symbol remained. The Biloxi Lighthouse, veteran of so many hurricanes in its 157-year history, was still standing. Its reassuring presence was transformed into an image of Mississippi's endurance.

Congress appropriated twelve thousand dollars for a Biloxi navigational beacon in March 1847, at the request of Representative Jefferson Davis. A one-acre tract of land was purchased from John Fayard and bids let for construction costs. Murray and Hazlehurst Vulcan Works, a Baltimore firm, was chosen to cast iron plates, which were then shipped down the Atlantic seaboard on the brig *General North*. A hollow cone of brick was built, enclosing an iron stairway, and the nine iron plates were then riveted together as an outer envelope. Nine brass lamps and reflectors were hung in the watch tower, sixty feet above the sand. When the oil lamps were lit, their reflection could be seen thirteen miles across the Mississippi Sound.

Marcellus J. Howard was appointed keeper of the Biloxi Light, earning four hundred dollars for each of the six years he served there. Senator Albert Gallatin Brown used his political clout to wrangle an unusual appointment after Howard's term. Mary Reynolds was an intriguing character, a widow or spinster who took in orphan children to raise in the lighthouse keeper's cottage. Her tenure was uneventful until the onset of the Civil War. She didn't feel threatened by the rare sight of Union ships, but was beset by trouble from local politicians and busybodies, prompting an angry letter from Reynolds to Governor John J. Pettus:

> With the request that you will pardon my informality in my letter, I beg leave to inform you that I am a woman entirely unprotected. I have for several years

The Biloxi Lighthouse's brick core and iron plates survived the destructive winds and storm surge of Hurricane Katrina.

past been the Keeper of the Light House at Biloxi, the small salary accruing from which has helped me to support a large family of orphan children . . . On the 18th of June last, the citizens of Biloxi ordered the light to be extinguished which was immediately done and shortly after others came and demanded the key of the Light Tower which has ever since remained in the hands of a Company calling themselves "Home Guards." At the time they took possession of the Tower it contained valuable Oil, the quantity being marked on my books. I have on several occasions seen disreputable characters taking out the oil in bottles. Today they carried away a large stone jug capable of containing several gallons. They may take also in the night as no one here appeared to have any authority over them. Their Captain, J. Fewell, is also Mayor of the City of Biloxi and if you would have the kindness to write him orders to have the oil measured and placed under my charge at the dwelling of the Light House I would be very grateful to you for so doing.

I write to you merely as a Light Keeper believing that injustice has been and is still doing here. I can give you unquestionable references as regards my character . . . I have ever faithfully performed the duties of Light Keeper in storm and sunshine attending it. I ascended the Tower at and after the last destructive storm [1860] when man stood appalled at the danger I encountered . . .

May I hope Gov. Pettus will see that I am again put in charge of the Light House Stores? Even in case these people as a Military Body should require the Light Tower as an observatory or for any other pur-

pose, they surely can have no right to carry away the oil for their private use.[38]

Mary Reynolds must have received some satisfaction from her letter, for she continued on as lighthouse keeper until 1866. Her replacement, Perry Younghans, died within a year of his appointment, and his wife, Maria, took over. For the next sixty-three years, Maria Younghans and her daughter, Miranda, kept the Biloxi light burning. They prevailed through hurricanes, damage from wayward pelicans, and the unrealized threat of German warboats. W. D. Thompson finally took over from the Younghans and then relinquished control of the lighthouse to the U.S. Coast Guard in 1939.

Automatic electric lights were installed in the high glass tower in the mid-1900s, and the position of lighthouse keeper vanished. One of America's first paved highways, the Old Spanish Trail, swept right past the old iron beacon, leaving it stranded on a median between four lanes of rushing traffic. Hurricane Camille destroyed the keeper's cottage in 1969, but was unable to bring down the ancient lighthouse itself.

In August 1968, the Biloxi Lighthouse was deeded to the City of Biloxi. It has achieved iconic status, an unchanging monument that has witnessed and withstood casino development, political turmoil, and the ravages of time. Its survival through Hurricane Katrina, which left so much of Biloxi and its neighboring cities in ruins, was nothing short of a miracle. Its light, which once guided brigs and schooners into the safe waters of Biloxi Bay, will now symbolize the rebirth of a strong and resurgent Mississippi Gulf Coast.

CHAPEL OF THE CROSS

TUCKED INTO A GROVE of ancient trees, hard by the bustle of Madison County's Highway 463, is a small Gothic chapel, a bit of medieval England seemingly misplaced in the Mississippi countryside. It was once the ecclesiastical anchor of a vast plantation, long vanished. Years of near-abandonment and the recent encroachment of Jackson's suburbs have threatened the old church, but it remains an oasis of Victorian calm in an otherwise hurried world.

The Chapel of the Cross was erected as a memorial to one of central Mississippi's earliest and most successful settlers. John Johnstone and his brothers first traveled to the new state in 1820, lured by the promise of vast Indian lands just begging to be bought and converted into prosperous plantations. The Johnstone brothers would trek back and forth between North Carolina and Mississippi for the next fifteen years, until John finally moved his family permanently to Madison County in 1835.

With his wife, Margaret, Johnstone settled near the village of Livingston. He accumulated over twenty-five hundred acres, along with land in DeSoto and Sunflower counties. An existing log cabin was enlarged and covered with siding, becoming the first Johnstone homeplace to be known as Annandale. Nearby, on a fourteen-hundred-acre plantation, elder daughter Frances and her husband would build the Italianate villa Ingleside.

The Johnstones were planning a palatial home for themselves and their younger daughter, Helen, when John died suddenly at age forty-seven. The indomitable Margaret soldiered on, hiring an architect and overseeing the building of the legendary Annandale, a forty-room Italianate mansion. It towered over rural Madison County like a castle, with its arches and bracketed eaves. Annandale would stand only until 1924, but Margaret's next project was equally beautiful and more enduring.

The building was completed and ready for consecration in 1852. Bishop William Mercer Green recorded the day in his journal:

Sunday, July 19, 1852 . . . I consecrated to the service of Almighty God the Chapel of the Cross. That beautiful and truly Church-like building was erected for the most part by Mrs. Margaret Johnstone near her residence in Madison County. The services were divided among the Clergy present, and seemed deeply to impress the congregation, many of whom had never witnessed anything of the kind before. The only thing to be regretted was the Church could not contain one half the persons in attendance. At the close of the service a bountiful and varied collation was served, sufficient for all—the bonded as well as the free. Together with this beautiful Temple, Mrs. Johnstone has given 10 acres of land surrounding the Church, which will not only keep at a distance any future possible disturbers of our worship, but will also afford, when desirable, a site for a rectory and a Parish school house.[39]

The Chapel of the Cross was conceived as a memorial to John Johnstone. After much consideration, Margaret chose the "Sketch of a First-Pointed Church" illustrated in English architect Frank Wills's *New York Ecclesiologist* of October 1849. The sketch featured a brick Gothic chapel with buttresses, a bellcote, and severely pointed windows. The asymmetrical door placement was characteristic of the English Gothic style.

Margaret put her slaves and hired artisans to work on the church in late 1849. For two years, they burned bricks, chopped down oak trees for hand-hewn beams, and fashioned doors from solid wood. Stained-glass windows, an Italian marble font, and a pipe organ were ordered from various cities and carried overland from the Mississippi River to the site.

For more than ten years, services in the chapel were held twice each Sunday, morning and evening. In the early

Previous page: The Chapel of the Cross's Gothic façade is based on a design by English architect Frank Wills.

Left: Legends from the Chapel of the Cross graveyard include the midnight burial of Henry Grey Vick.

Right: Madison County's Chapel of the Cross was built by Margaret Johnstone as a memorial to her husband.

service, white parishioners were seated at the front and slaves to the rear and along the aisles. At night, the seating arrangement was reversed.

Two years before the Civil War brought the idyllic early years of the chapel to a close, it was the scene for one of the most legendary funerals in Mississippi history. Helen Johnstone, Margaret and John's younger daughter, had enjoyed a long engagement to Henry Grey Vick, nephew of Vicksburg's founder. The wedding was planned for Helen's twenty-first birthday, on May 21, 1859. While final decorations were laid out in Annandale and in the chapel, Vick left for a quick business trip to New Orleans. Accounts of what transpired there vary, but it is known that he exchanged angry words with another man. True to the tenor of the time, a challenge was laid down and the two men met on the dueling field in Mobile. Early on the morning of May 17, Henry Vick died of a single pistol shot.

The sad news was relayed to Madison County by courier. Hugh Miller Thompson II recalled his grandmother's description of the day and its aftermath: "Mrs. Johnstone, Helen and Margaret were in the parlor of Ingleside arranging decorations. Someone, probably a servant, came in and said there was a man on horseback riding fast up the road. Mrs. Johnstone went out to meet the rider. He dismounted and handed her a telegram. She opened the envelope and read its contents. As she turned toward the house Helen and Margaret came down the walk to meet her. She was chalk white and staggered a little as she walked . . . Helen took the telegram from her. When she read it she screamed, 'No! God, No!' . . . My grandmother picked up the telegram from where it had fallen and read, 'Henry Vick killed today May 17 in a duel at Mobile, Alabama. Will bring body to Vicksburg on earliest steamer.'"[40]

Three long days passed before Henry Vick's body arrived in Vicksburg. Hasty arrangements were made for his burial in the churchyard at the Chapel of the Cross, where wedding decorations were being pulled down and stored. Hugh Thompson II recounted the scene, handed down in family lore: "Word came that the body would arrive in Vicksburg by boat on the 20th day of May about noon. Then there was the fifty mile drive to the Chapel of the Cross. A crowd of mourners gathered at the Chapel that evening, May 20, 1859. When the body arrived near midnight men were stationed with lighted torches along the driveway and in the vicinity of the grave to provide light for the funeral . . . Vick's casket was packed in charcoal and coffee . . . The box in which the casket was packed was very large. As my grandmother said, it was like a 'piano box.' Because of the size of the box, the body was not taken into the Chapel. Services were held at graveside by Bishop Green, Dr. Sansom, Rector of the Chapel, and priests who had known Vick. Grandmother said it was a scene she would never forget."[41]

The bereft Helen Johnstone would pass into legend as "the bride of Annandale," a sad figure who pined away, wandering the graveyard behind the chapel. Reality was far different: Helen soon married Dr. George C. Harris, who served as wartime rector at the church and also as a Confederate chaplain. They would enjoy a long and happy marriage, eventually adding one more piece to Mississippi's architectural heritage. Their home, Mont Helena, still sits atop an Indian mound in Sharkey County.

Helen's life may have turned out for the best, but the years following the eerie midnight burial were difficult ones for the Chapel of the Cross. Wartime depression and economic despair led to a steep decline in the number of active parishioners. Bishop Green chanced by the site in 1867: "I stopped a moment to see the 'Chapel of the Cross' and was grieved at heart in contrasting its present deserted and decaying condition with what it was a few years ago. It was then surrounded by friends and founders, and blessed with frequent ministrations, black and white sharing equally in the instructions of a faithful pastor. Now, strangers are pressing their boundaries close up to the sacred enclosure of its dead; mold is fast growing on its walls, and from Lord's day to Lord's day no track is seen of any one going up to this House of Prayer."[42]

The next fifty years would find no positive change in the condition of the church. In 1911, theology student Valentine Sessions discovered the decrepit chapel and began holding services there as time and studies allowed. The descendants of the Johnstone and Britton families were enlisted, and work was initiated on restoration and stabilization. A new roof was installed and the windows replaced. Reverend Sessions would stay on for thirty years, dedicated to the little chapel he had stumbled upon as a young man.

After Reverend Sessions was gone, the chapel once again faded from most people's memories and concerns. The local Children of the American Revolution chapter made cosmetic improvements in the 1950s, but there was no active congregation to enliven the sanctuary. Ghost stories led teenagers and college students to make late night forays into the churchyard, but the still-evident beauty of the church must have protected it from mindless vandalism.

Increased interest in the 1970s brought a National Register of Historic Places nomination to the chapel. As prosperous suburbs developed north of Jackson, new worshippers found the ancient church and devoted themselves to maintaining its integrity and atmosphere. Each year, the grounds are packed with visitors and parishioners at A Day in the Country, which brings the church and the memory of Margaret Johnstone back to life.

CHAPEL OF THE CROSS RECTORY

JACKSON'S MANSHIP HOUSE is a carefully preserved example of Gothic Revival architecture, its carved vergeboards, steeply pitched roofline, and pointed gables prime elements of the mid-1800s style. The house was based on "Design XXIV" in Andrew Jackson Downing's 1850 *Architecture of Country Houses*, the bible of the Gothic style. Downing strongly emphasized rural, pastoral settings for the homes built to his specifications, and when the Manship House was erected, it fulfilled those expectations. Over a century and a half, though, Jackson has swallowed the lot and erased the intended ambience of a country villa.

Oddly enough, a carbon copy of the Manship House still exists, surrounded by the nature that Andrew Downing preferred. Several years before Henry Manship laid the foundation for his Jackson home, Margaret Johnstone was overseeing the construction of a rectory for her Episcopal church, Madison County's Chapel of the Cross. She had financed the building of the chapel as a memorial to her late husband, and the rectory was the crowning touch to the property.

Set in rolling fields just west of the chapel, the rectory is a one-story frame cottage with an imposing, steeply arched central gable. Elaborately carved woodwork outlines the gable and side porches. In a variation from the Manship House, an oriel window is centered in the pediment.

Mrs. Johnstone's hopes for the Chapel of the Cross and the rectory were derailed by the onset of the Civil War. Following consecration of the church in 1852, only three rectors occupied the house. John F. Young, Henry Sansom, and Benjamin Smyser must have felt that they had been led to the most idyllic pastorate in Mississippi, but they were not replaced during the chaos of the war years. The chapel and the rectory fell into disuse.

Local resident John Daniel Mann rescued the rectory with his purchase of it in 1866. Several generations of his family and plantation managers occupied the Gothic cot-

Built to serve as the Chapel of the Cross's rectory, this house is based on the same plan as Jackson's Manship House.

tage for the next one hundred years, adapting it to fit the needs of modern life. The Mann family lost ownership during the Depression, and for several years the house sat vacant.

In the late 1940s, Lee DeWeese, great-great-grandson of Daniel Mann, and his wife, Pat, purchased the house and embarked on a long-term restoration. Mrs. DeWeese was overwhelmed at first. "There was hardly any paint on it and there was an old barbed wire fence around it to keep the cattle out. Enormous chunks of plaster were out of the walls, with even more plaster falling off. There were screened galleries all around the house, the foundation was sagging and it [the house] was vacant . . . We moved into a front bedroom to live, while the rest of the house was just gutted . . . The walls came down, the fireplaces (which were in nearly every room) came out, the chimneys came out, and we lowered the ceilings from 14 to 12 feet."[43]

The DeWeese family faithfully maintained the old rectory as their home for almost fifty years. The property was sold in 2000 and donated back to the newly revitalized Chapel of the Cross congregation. As with the church, it stands as a charming reminder of a quieter time amid the bustle of modern-day Madison County.

LONGFELLOW HOUSE

OF ALL MISSISSIPPI's fabled mansions, probably none has led a more varied and treacherous existence than Longfellow House. Built by slave traders, repeatedly abandoned and threatened with demolition, and battered by some of America's worst natural disasters, this grand old house has survived many a close call.

The home once known as Bellevue was built during the 1850s, the peak period for New Orleans and Mobile residents' quest for Mississippi coastal real estate. All that is known of the original owner, Daniel Smith Graham, is that he made his fortune through slave trading, a less-than-admired profession even in the antebellum South.

The house the Grahams built was designed to optimize the climate of the coastal region. Consisting of two stories with a raised basement, it features elaborate Greek Revival detailing and the "open arms" stairway so often seen on Gulf Coast mansions. Doric and Corinthian columns support a full entablature, and three dormers pierce the gabled roofline. Twin chimneys add to the symmetrical appearance of the house.

In its first fifty years, Bellevue went through numerous owners and even served as a girls' school for a time. Greenville banker W. A. Pollock bought the property, including the house and forty acres, in 1902. Following his death in 1938, Ingalls Shipbuilding, Pascagoula's largest industry, acquired the site. It was converted to a resort and private club, with fine dining facilities, a small golf course, and clay tennis courts. Generations of Jackson County children swam in the pool or lounged on the long pier, phoning in to the house for orders of pink lemonade and hamburgers. White-coated waiters with extraordinary balance would then bicycle down the pier, trays held high with summer treats.

At some point, Bellevue became known as Longfellow House. Legend held that Henry Wadsworth Longfellow vacationed in Pascagoula and was inspired to write "The

Building of the Ship" during his stay there. While the poem does refer to Pascagoula, there is no firm evidence that the poet ever set foot in Bellevue. Nevertheless, it was his name that would come to be most closely associated with the mansion.

As decades passed and Ingalls lost interest in maintaining the Longfellow House estate, the property began to decline. Restaurant and bed-and-breakfast schemes were unsuccessful. The house was slated for demolition when it was purchased by Richard and Diane Scruggs in 1993. They invested more than one million dollars in renovation and then graciously donated the site to the University of Mississippi Foundation.

Ole Miss was in the process of seeking buyers for Longfellow House when Hurricane Katrina hit in August 2005. Most of the antebellum homes along Pascagoula's Beach Boulevard were destroyed, and Longfellow House was buffeted with damaging winds and a massive surge of water through the raised basement. The grand stairway, so long associated with the house, was ripped apart. Once again, this survivor of numerous threats was under a cloud, with its own future and that of the coast uncertain.

In June 2006, Drs. Randy and Tracy Roth purchased the Longfellow House estate, with intentions of restoring it as a family home. The basement level will be repaired and the front stairs replaced exactly as they were before the storm. Longfellow House will once again serve as a homeplace, for the first time in more than sixty-five years.

Longfellow House, originally known as Bellevue, was for many years the centerpiece of a famous Gulf Coast resort.

POINT LEFLORE

THE TALLAHATCHIE RIVER starts as a shallow stream near Blue Mountain, no wider than the myriad unnamed creeks which flow out of the Appalachian foothills of northeast Mississippi. As this "River of Rocks" snakes toward the Delta, it absorbs smaller waterways and then disappears into Sardis Reservoir. It reappears as a roaring torrent, tumbling across the spillway, and picks up speed and depth as it cuts through the Delta, twisting back and forth and finally sweeping along the northern edge of Greenwood.

The Yalobusha River takes a shorter, calmer course from Grenada Lake, down the loess bluffs along the Delta and slowly toward Greenwood. The Choctaws named it "Abundance of Tadpoles," appropriate for a friendlier, welcoming stream. Those Indians must have seen the narrow triangle of land where the quiet Yalobusha slides into the Tallahatchie, giving birth to the Yazoo, their famed "River of Death."

Where the Tallahatchie, Yalobusha, and Yazoo rivers converge, Greenwood Leflore built his short-lived namesake town.

The exact point where one river is transformed into another is indefinable. But the spit of land closest to this geologic oddity was well known to Greenwood Leflore, who acquired it as part of the vast acreage ceded to him by the Treaty of Dancing Rabbit Creek. Just a few years after he signed that agreement, most of his tribe was exiled to Oklahoma Territory, and Leflore was a rich man. He planted cotton in the rich bottomlands of the eastern Delta and shipped the bales out at John Williams's port on the Yazoo.

Williams Landing often saw dozens of boats lined up on the south bank of the Yazoo, bringing in supplies and reloading with immense bales of cotton destined for Vicksburg and New Orleans. Each bale was worth a small fortune, and Greenwood Leflore was understandably furious when much of his crop was left in the rain to ruin. Most planters would have simply fumed or perhaps sued, but Leflore had the financial wherewithal to ratchet his revenge up to a higher level. He sent his slaves to clear the underbrush and forest a few miles upriver, at the spot where the three rivers converged. Point Leflore was born out of anger, and it was successful enough that it soon boasted its own hotel, a cotton gin, and several stores. To ease the carriage ride from his home at Teoc, Leflore built a "corduroy" road, fourteen miles of logs split and laid side by side all the way to the town.

For several years, the twin towns of Williams Landing and Point Leflore competed for cotton and riverboat traffic. But as Greenwood Leflore's attention shifted to his rising Italianate manor, Malmaison, Point Leflore began to decline. Insightful Williams Landing promoters, eager to reclaim their monopoly on river traffic, devised the scheme of renaming their community Greenwood. Flattery was an effective tool in this case; Point Leflore was doomed. The Choctaw chief turned his back on his experiment, leaving it to the annual floods and creeping forest. The buildings crumbled and vanished.

As the Civil War crept into the Delta, Point Leflore again caught an innovative man's attention. General U. S. Grant was desperate to reach and subdue Vicksburg, but he could not succeed in a direct attack on that town's bluff fortifications. He proposed a complicated scheme to dynamite the levee at Yazoo Pass, float warships into Moon Lake and then bring them down a series of Delta streams and rivers until they reached Vicksburg by the back door.

Grant's plan was doomed from the beginning. He had no grasp of the narrow, tortuous waterways he was navigating. Progress was glacial, and Confederate snipers happily perched in cypress trees along the way, tormenting the sluggish boats as they crept toward Greenwood. Nor did Grant realize that the fabled *Star of the West*, the first ship to draw fire in Charleston Harbor, had been stripped of its engines, turned sideways and sunk in the Tallahatchie just a few miles above Point Leflore. On the actual point, backup earthworks were erected on the ruins of Greenwood Leflore's short-lived town. The Thirty-fifth Mississippi Infantry and an artillery company piled up dirt and trees, topping them with cotton bales.

When the Union flotilla slowed to negotiate the Tallahatchie's hairpin turn, they found the river blocked by the ruined *Star of the West*. Forced to retreat the way they came, they never reached Point Leflore. Random troops skirmished briefly in a field just across the Yalobusha from the point. The eager Confederate gunners hurled the shells of their six-pound gun at the First Missouri Light Artillery, which responded with thirteen rounds of their own. It was a tiny, inconsequential battle in a war that was soon to be decided at Vicksburg.

In the century and a half since 1863, Point Leflore has receded into wilderness. Deer tracks are ubiquitous, and snakes are more in abundance than the Choctaws' tadpoles. No trace remains of Greenwood Leflore's exercise in spite, and only the most diligent trekkers can trace the mounds that mark the Confederate earthworks.

COTESWORTH

As north Mississippi filled up with eager settlers in the early-to-mid-1800s, small towns and villages evolved to serve their needs. Some flourished; others quickly wilted and today are only remembered by indirect references, such as Old Salem Road or Wyatt Landing.

Carrollton was one of the survivors, claiming the hills above the Mississippi Delta and providing a relatively disease-free home for planters farming below Valley Hill. A few miles to the northeast, Grenada grew out of the symbolic wedding of two feuding communities, Tullahoma and Pittsburg. A stagecoach road wound between Carrollton and Grenada.

Traveling in that day was a challenge, even for short distances. Roads, at best, were hard-packed dirt and, at worst, muddy quagmires. The trip from Carrollton to Grenada could easily consume the better part of a day. Overnight accommodations were scarce and rudimentary. The only known inn between the two towns was a two-story wooden structure, with just two rooms on each floor.

Its name, if it ever officially had one, has been lost. But it would be transformed into one of the most unique houses in antebellum Mississippi.

James Zachariah George, a successful young Carrollton lawyer, bought the inn in the years preceding the Civil War. George had moved to Mississippi from Georgia as a child and studied law with a Carrollton mentor, passing the bar at age twenty. He married well and had a house full of children, and the sturdy old inn on the Grenada Road caught his attention. He purchased it, along with five hundred rolling acres of pasture land, and set about making it into a home.

The four original rooms of the inn were joined by two additional formal rooms on the front. George then added a flat-roofed portico with giant-order square columns and a simple entablature. A cantilevered balcony with an ornate iron balustrade was hung over the deep veranda. The clapboard siding was scored to resemble the more elegant idea of stone. On the gabled ends, full-height chimneys were

added to service the fireplaces, but their asymmetrical placement attested to the altered origins of the home.

Several years after the massive renovation was completed, J. Z. George added a one-story wing on the east side, ingeniously incorporating a bedroom with screened porches surrounding it. He named the completed house Cotesworth, in honor of an old Georgia friend and jurist.

The George family had barely settled into Cotesworth when J. Z. was called away as one of Carroll County's delegates to the 1861 Secession Convention. He voted in favor of the Ordinance of Secession and soon afterwards joined a volunteer regiment headed for war. He would rise to the rank of colonel in the Confederate Army, but his

Left: J. Z. George's Carroll County mansion, Cotesworth, has passed through several generations of his descendants.

Right: Cotesworth's hexagonal library contains J. Z. George's law books and copies of *Congressional Record*.

greatest service to Mississippi came in the difficult years of Reconstruction. It was J. Z. George's voice that would calm a state teetering on the brink of self-annihilation.

Mississippi was placed under Federal occupation for years following Appomattox. "Carpetbaggers" and "scalawags" joined newly liberated blacks in dominating state politics for almost a decade. By 1875, tempers were fraying. White Democrats were marshalling their numbers to reclaim power, by violent means if necessary. Riots had already broken out in Vicksburg, Yazoo City, and Clinton. Governor Adelbert Ames was in a panic, telegraphing Washington with desperate pleas for Federal troops before the elections. President Grant, ready to put the turmoil of Reconstruction behind him, refused to back up Ames.

Governor Ames ordered the state militia, largely composed of freedmen, to be ready to march into the troubled cities. Incensed whites, spurred on by rabblerousing editorialists in local newspapers, were primed and ready for the confrontation. A full-scale race war was looming for Mississippi. L. Q. C. Lamar summed up the ominous atmosphere of the time: "I think the future of Mississippi is very dark. Ames has it dead . . . May God help us."[44]

J. Z. George had risen to prominence in state political circles. In 1875, he was chairman of the Democratic Election Committee, charged with sweeping whites back into positions of power. He recognized the brewing violence as an excuse for Governor Ames to pull the hated Federal troops back into Mississippi and dominate the elections. Gathering eleven other Democratic leaders, he requested an emergency meeting with the governor. Ames, sensing political and personal Armageddon, agreed.

The meeting took place in the parlor of the Governor's Mansion. Time was a critical element; George knew that large groups of angry men were massing in Rankin, Hinds, Yazoo, and Warren counties, ready to destroy the Ames militias and any innocent blacks who got in their way. George laid the situation out for Ames, guaranteeing peaceful elections if the governor would recall and disband the military units. Backed into a corner, Ames agreed to recall but not to disband the militias. Accepting the compromise, George hastily sent word around the state that the crisis had been defused. Grumbling but placated, the Democratic mobs went home.

George was hailed as a hero, all the more so when he led the Democratic party to overwhelming victories in the November 1875 elections. He may have been tempted to retire at that point to Cotesworth, but his legal skills were needed in the still-evolving New South. Narrowly passed over for a Senate seat that went to L. Q. C. Lamar, he was appointed to the state supreme court, where he served briefly as chief justice. In 1881, he was finally elected to Congress and served there for the last sixteen years of his life. His efforts to establish the Department of Agriculture and pass the Sherman Antitrust Act earned him the national nickname of "the Great Commoner."

George finally earned some time at home in Carrollton when he was chosen to write the 1890 Mississippi Constitution. In the parlor at Cotesworth, a small desk was his workspace for long months, as he labored to draft a code of laws that would carry Mississippi into the next century.

The state still operates under George's 1890 Constitution, although in a much amended form. That document has changed much more than Cotesworth, which remains in the George family and serves as a comfortable country home. The desk is still in the parlor, and most of J. Z. George's law books and copies of *Congressional Record* can be found on the shelves in the hexagonal library near the house. In the U. S. Capitol's Statuary Hall, a marble likeness of J. Z. George memorializes the man who led Mississippi out of the dark days of Reconstruction.

L. Q. C. Lamar House

In the more than two hundred years of American history, only a handful of citizens have served in all three branches of the federal government. Oddly enough, L. Q. C. Lamar, Mississippi's single representative in that exclusive club, actually drafted the ordinance which took his state out of the union. Thirteen years later, he delivered a congressional oration which many credit for pulling the fractured nation back together. During the tumultuous years that separated those two occasions, Lamar made his home in an unassuming cottage on Oxford's Fourteenth Street.

Lucius Quintus Cincinnatus Lamar was born in Georgia in 1825. He graduated from Emory University and passed the bar in his native state in 1847. Along with picking up his law degree, Lamar also courted and married Virginia Longstreet, the daughter of Emory's president. When her father, Augustus Baldwin Longstreet, was lured to Mississippi to serve as the first chancellor of the brand-new University of Mississippi, Lamar and his new bride

followed. It was a fortuitous move for the young couple and also, ultimately, for their adopted state.

The Lamar family set down roots in Oxford, a farming community which was just beginning to see the economic benefits of hosting the state's flagship college. Lawyers found their practices lucrative and many dabbled in politics on the side. L. Q. C. Lamar sided with the opponents of the Compromise of 1850 and won his political reputation in a spirited debate with gubernatorial candidate Henry Foote on the Lafayette County Courthouse square. He went on to win election to the Senate in 1857, defeating Whig candidate James L. Alcorn.

As the country edged toward dissolution and war, Lamar vociferously defended southern states' rights and slavery. Following the election of Abraham Lincoln and South Carolina's secession, Lamar surrendered his Senate seat and dashed home to Mississippi. He was chosen to draft the Ordinance of Secession, which was readily signed

by his fellow secession conveners and presented to a cheering crowd from the balcony of the Old Capitol.

Mississippi exited the Union and readied for war. For his part, Lamar organized a volunteer infantry regiment, which elected him colonel. He was later appointed envoy to Russia by Confederate president Jefferson Davis.

The war soon landed on Lamar's Oxford doorstep. The buildings of the university were turned into hospitals following the Battle of Shiloh, and vengeful Union troops would eventually burn much of Oxford to the ground. Lamar returned to find the courthouse and square in ruins, the homes of many of his friends gutted, and his adopted state in shambles. He reopened his law office, preached sectional reconciliation, and worked to promote the rights of the slaves that he had previously labored to keep servile. When the university resumed operations, he

was appointed professor of metaphysics and then professor of law.

Lamar and his wife had made their home since the prewar days at Solitude Plantation, near Abbeville. Finding it in ruins after Federal occupation, they moved to the old Barger home on Fourteenth Street, conveniently located next door to Mrs. Lamar's parents. The single-story frame cottage, topped by a hipped roof with two chimneys, featured a wide center hall and four 20′ x 20′ rooms. Front and rear porticoes mirrored each other. The interior plaster walls were stenciled with decorative scenes and the man-

Left: The Oxford–Lafayette County Heritage Foundation is undertaking a multimillion dollar renovation of Lamar's home.

Right: L. Q. C. Lamar moved to this Fourteenth Street Greek Revival cottage in Oxford after his plantation home was destroyed.

tels were plain and functional. It was a simple, utilitarian house, in no way competing with the fine mansions scattered around Oxford and Lafayette County.

Lamar's practical nature was evident in his academic career as well as his choice of homes. He instituted the case method of legal studies while teaching at the university, an innovation that was eventually adopted by most law schools throughout America. When Radical Republicans took control of Mississippi's government, he resigned his position at the law school, fearing changes at the college which he could not tolerate.

Lamar returned to Congress in 1872 and found the nation's capital still torn with sectional differences and postwar bitterness. When Massachusetts senator Charles Sumner died in 1874, Lamar stood in Congress to deliver a eulogy. To a spellbound audience, Lamar memorialized the fire-breathing abolitionist who had fought against everything the South stood for in the 1850s. He pleaded for reconciliation and forgiveness, and his words rocketed around the country by telegraph. America was ready for healing, and Lamar's words had initiated the process. Thirteen years after he penned the Ordinance of Secession, Lamar's oratorical talents had pulled the country back together.

His reputation as a scholar and legal expert caught the attention of President Grover Cleveland, who appointed Lamar secretary of the interior and, a few years later, Supreme Court justice. It had taken twenty years for a southerner to rejoin the nation's highest court, and Lamar took on the task with the same spirit of compromise he had shown throughout his career.

Traveling back and forth from Oxford to Washington was tedious and difficult, and in 1888, Justice Lamar sold the Fourteenth Street house to his daughter, Fannie Mayes. Five years later, he died in Georgia, en route to the Mississippi Gulf Coast. He was buried in his native state but later reinterred in Oxford.

The Lamar house passed through a number of families and alterations. The rear porch was removed and the surrounding woods gradually took over the lawn and hid the house from the street. Near ruin, it was purchased by the Oxford–Lafayette County Heritage Foundation in 2004 and is undergoing a multimillion dollar restoration.

JACINTO COURTHOUSE

IN THE FAR NORTHEAST CORNER of Mississippi, an area that could have easily been part of Alabama if surveyors had jogged their lines just a few miles to the west, sits a quiet, dignified courthouse. Like many of the state's county seats of political power, it's situated on a square, but the stores and businesses and bustle are long gone. Jacinto is all but a ghost town, a relic of Mississippi's earliest pioneer days.

Ten counties were formed after the Treaty of Pontotoc in 1832. The Chickasaw Indians moved west and left Mississippi with the territory which would become Itawamba, DeSoto, Tunica, Panola, Tippah, Pontotoc, Lafayette, Marshall, Chickasaw, and Tishomingo counties. The last was the largest, a huge swath of land encompassing more than twelve hundred square miles. Only five thousand hardy souls lived in Tishomingo County when the land office opened; they were scattered from the borders with Tennessee and Alabama to what are now Booneville and Ripley.

With such an enormous amount of land to control, the board of police (forerunner to today's supervisors) requested that the county seat be located in as central a site as possible. Armistead Barton donated sixty acres of his cropland near Rienzi, the board laid out a county square, and the tiny community of Cincinnati was born. Fifty-three town lots were sold on October 11, 1836, leading to an influx of new citizens, including lawyers, doctors, businessmen, and preachers.

A wave of national pride following the Mexican War led to unusual names in places that had no Spanish heritage. Cincinnati became Jacinto, honoring the victors in the battle of San Jacinto and forever linking the town with the Spanish word for hyacinth. It continued to grow, and by 1836, a log courthouse was up on the square, at a cost of less than two hundred dollars.

In 1837, the board contracted for a jail, to be built for four thousand dollars. This brick structure must have led to some embarrassment in comparison with the tiny court-

house, and it soon came to house all branches of government as well as prisoners. It was completed in 1840 and served until 1854, when the building that has come to be known as the Jacinto Courthouse replaced it.

Tishomingo County in the 1850s was prosperous, despite its relative isolation from the rest of Mississippi. Ripley, Eastport, Corinth, and Iuka were all growing towns, each looking to Jacinto for their government business. Residents wanted a fine and permanent county building that would rival those going up in Holly Springs, Columbus, and Aberdeen. The plan that was accepted called for a 40' x 50' brick building, two stories tall, with an octagonal belfry. Four offices would occupy the first floor, with a courtroom and two jury rooms above. Exterior walls were to be eighteen inches thick. The total cost was a bit less than seven thousand dollars, with an extra twenty-five dollars appropriated for a lightning rod. In keeping with local traditions of frugality, the board handed over a check for the entire amount the day it was finished.

In late 1859, the Tishomingo County Agricultural and Mechanical Society sponsored the first Jacinto Fair. Building on their success, they held another one in 1860 but found interest had shifted to war talk by 1861. Jacinto would see only peripheral action during the Civil War, escaping the devastating battles nearby at Shiloh, Corinth, Iuka, and Brice's Crossroads. County government continued to provide services and relief for those directly affected by the conflict.

Reconstruction was not as kind to Tishomingo and Jacinto. A carpetbagger-dominated legislature split the county in 1870, forming Alcorn, Prentiss, and a new, much-diminished Tishomingo County from the original. Corinth took over government functions for Alcorn County, Booneville became the county seat of Prentiss County and Iuka was awarded the courthouse for Tishomingo. Jacinto, already geographically challenged, was left high and dry.

The courthouse was abandoned as an unneeded relic. The former county clerk, in exchange for laboriously copying records to be transferred to Corinth, was given the title to the building. He opened the Jacinto Male Academy in the high-ceilinged rooms. The school met with some success and was active until 1908. By that time, most of the town of Jacinto had dried up and its population was in freefall. The Methodist church utilized the old courthouse until 1960, when the newly formed Jacinto Foundation purchased it. In 1969, it was formally dedicated as a museum and educational center, and it continues to serve that purpose today. The foundation sponsors a Fourth of July fair each summer, attracting hundreds of picnickers and politicians to the square and briefly bringing the old courthouse back to life.

When a Reconstruction legislature carved Tishomingo County into three new counties, the Jacinto Courthouse was abandoned as a government center.

St. John's Episcopal Church

Lake Washington is a long, curving oxbow, stretching parallel to the Mississippi River, which carved it out and then abandoned it eons ago. It's a dark, tree-lined, faintly ominous body of water, its cypress knees and Spanish moss providing a hint of the forbidding Delta that intrepid settlers encountered in the early 1800s.

Washington County was established in 1826, formed from Hinds County and Yazoo County lands just nine years after Mississippi became a state. It wasn't a real estate developer's dream. Unlike much of Mississippi, with inviting hills and rolling pastures, this was a wild and untamed corner, more densely populated with bears, water moccasins, and "mosquitoes the size of bumblebees"[45] than with people. Every spring, the myriad Delta rivers jumped their banks, laying down ever more topsoil but also obliterating any hardwon agricultural gains. In truly unfortunate years,

the mighty Mississippi roared into the county, and more than one home was swept away by the great river's wrath. As late as 1857, state geologist Lewis Harper was hedging his bets on the region's future: "This alluvial plain is still a wilderness; the prejudice of its unfitness for cultivation has only lately subsided, and the axe of the woodman scarcely begun its ravages."[46]

With time, the swamps were drained, trees felled, and a vibrant but isolated agricultural economy developed. Families from the Carolinas and Kentucky bought land near Lake Washington and built a handful of fine houses before the Civil War. The county seat at Princeton, though never more than a crossroads, offered a few stores and a site from which government could function.

Organized religion took a backseat to the basic necessities of life in this rough frontier. Episcopal bishop James Otey rode through the Delta in 1844 and again in 1847. "We arrived at Mr. George Skipwith's, in the neighborhood of Lake Washington, and the next day administered

the Holy Communion to a sick person, a member of the Church, who in a few days after was gathered to her rest in peace . . . Rode through the rain and over an exceedingly muddy plain for nine miles to Princeton. Here we gathered ten or a dozen people in the old Court House, to whom I preached, after prayers had been offered by Rev. Dr. McLeod. The interest in behalf of the Church in the neighborhood has so increased, that a sufficient sum has now been subscribed for the erection of a church, which will probably be built and made ready for occupation by the fall of this year."[47]

Bishop Otey was overly optimistic on the building timetable. The Parish of St. John's was formally organized in 1848, incorporating the Church of the Crucifixion at Ivanhoe (Issaquena County) and St. John's Church on Lake Washington. One year later, William Mercer Green was appointed first bishop of the Diocese of Mississippi, and it was under his leadership that the small congregation at Glen Allan would start their building program.

Planter Jonathon McCaleb donated several acres of his vast Greenfield Plantation for the site of the proposed St. John's chapel. Bishop Green made frequent visits on horseback, encouraging the parishioners as they worked toward a permanent church. January 1855 found him once again in Washington County: "On Sunday, the 28th, I preached at Lake Washington and confirmed three persons. The congregation, though not large, filled the temporary place of worship in which we were assembled. The

A 1904 tornado destroyed the empty church, leaving an outline in ruins on the shores of Lake Washington.

beautiful Gothic church, begun by this liberal people last summer, will be, when completed, one of the most finished and tasty structures, not only in our Diocese, but in the whole South-west."[48]

Bishop Green paid particular care to the spiritual well-being of the slaves in this corner of the Delta. He must have been aware of the talents of Jesse Crowell, who worked on the Frederick Turnbull plantation. Crowell labored for months on the chapel, fashioning the millwork and pews and carving elaborate leaf and fern designs into the communion rail and altar.

When finally completed and consecrated on April 5, 1857, St. John's was a masterful creation. Tiny in comparison to the English Gothic parish churches on which it was modeled, it stood like a miniature jewel overlooking the dark waters of Lake Washington. Peaked gables, arched stained-glass windows, and a square bell tower with buttresses all evoked the medieval British countryside. The day of its consecration began as a typical warm, windy Delta spring day but gradually deteriorated into a howling maelstrom of rain, sleet, and snow. Perhaps this was an omen of the difficult years the church would face and its ultimate demise at the hands of nature.

St. John's was the only organized church in the Glen Allan area, and it enjoyed its monopoly by welcoming all comers, black and white, in the few years left before the Civil War. That conflict brought occasional skirmishes and destruction of property to the western Delta, and many of the church's members left for service or safer lands. As the needs of the Confederacy increased, congregations were often called upon to remove their stained-glass windows and provide the lead tracery for conversion into bullets. St. John's parishioners did this, certainly expecting to replace the windows within months.

That never happened. In the economically depressed Reconstruction years, the congregation dwindled and the chapel stood exposed to the weather. By 1869, just twelve years after the wild and windy consecration day, Bishop Green reluctantly declared St. John's to be unfit for worship. He visited again in 1882, and was saddened by the decay: "I rode to the church and found it a ruin indeed, though a beautiful one . . ."[49]

The church sat empty and forlorn for another twenty years. The Delta had recovered and prospered with the completion of levees and the coming of the railroad, and money was once again plentiful on Lake Washington. Ambitious plans were laid to renovate and reconsecrate the old church. A faded black-and-white photo taken around 1900 shows full-skirted ladies and straw-hatted gentlemen picnicking in front of the church.

That would be one of the last good days for an architectural gem that saw little but misfortune in its existence. In 1904, a spring tornado roared across the Mississippi River and caught the windowless building full force, hurling its bricks, pews, and Jesse Crowell's artwork through the neighboring cotton fields. All that remained were remnants of the outer walls and the bell tower, which have stood for a century as a reminder of the promise of St. John's.

Falkner-Gary House

In a famous but faded 1904 photograph, seven-year-old William Falkner sits astride his spotted pony, looking confident and serious even at that young age. His younger brothers, Murry and Jack, are seated on porch steps, each clutching the reins of smaller ponies. Cousin Sallie Murry Wilkins claims the tail end of one set of reins.

Behind the children is the front porch of a house that was then almost fifty years old. The brick sidewalk, broad front steps, screen door with transoms and sidelights, and the arched gingerbread trim and balustrades all mark the house as the one where the Falkner boys lived with their parents from 1902 until 1905. Were they still alive, they would recognize that house a century later, still intact with its unique woodwork and large, comfortable rooms.

The house on Buchanan Street was built by an Oxford clothier, James Trigg, in 1855. Trigg was a Kentucky native whose educational pursuits had led him to Princeton before he made his way down to Mississippi. He built the Carpenter Gothic home, with its wide central hallway and four adjoining rooms, on the rear of a huge lot backed by deep woods and pastures.

Six years later, Mr. Trigg sold the house to grocer Robert E. Doyle. Doyle must not have incurred the wrath of the Union troops rampaging through Oxford in 1864; many houses were destroyed in those dark days, but not the cottage on Buchanan Street. Following the war, Oxford rebuilt and Robert Doyle remodeled. Admiring the increasingly ornate fashions of the postwar era, he had fanciful wooden arches carved and installed on the front porch.

In 1887, the house was purchased by J. W. T. Falkner, son of a legendary Ripley railroad developer. Falkner was a larger-than-life character, successful in both business and politics, and he provided his less-than-ambitious son Murry with a series of railroad jobs. When the elder Falkner sold the family railroad in 1902, Murry was forced to move from New Albany to Oxford and take over his father's livery stable and cottonseed oil mill. By that time, J. W. T. Falkner had finished a mansion known as "the Big

House" on University Avenue. That freed up the Buchanan Street home for Murry, his wife, and three young sons.

The Falkners moved to Oxford in September 1902, just before their eldest son, William, turned five. They would live in the charming old house for three years, and that time was fondly remembered by both of William's younger brothers. John Falkner wrote of their turn-of-the-century life there:

> Our new home had a big pasture for the stock. Our lot was four hundred feet wide and a thousand deep. It was divided down the middle and one-half was pasture and barn lot and the house was on the other half, about five hundred feet back from the street. The whole was enclosed with a crisscross pattern fence and a like one divided pasture from front yard. I can remember Dad, arms crossed on the top rail, looking at his horses on the other side, and Bill and Jack and me, climbed up beside him, watching the horses too. From just behind our lot stretched a half mile to the railroad that linked Oxford and the University . . . A bridle path through the woods where we lived to the oil mill and Dad used to ride back and forth to work and let us ride with him. Bill and Jack had their own ponies, Shetlands, but I was too young to have one of my own.[50]

Murry Falkner's fondest memories were of a trusted family retainer. "There was one other member of our

household—Mammy Callie Barr, who came to us shortly after we arrived in Oxford and continued as an honored member of the family until her death forty years later. Mammy had a formidable imagination, a good memory of the 'old days,' and kept Bill, John and me (and later Dean) spellbound with her stories. Surely from her came many of Bill's writings about events in Lafayette County, especially those dealing with whites and blacks."[51]

The house had changed stylistically from its 1855 origins, but in 1904 it still lacked modern conveniences. "There

Left: As a five-year-old boy, William Falkner moved to his grandfather's Oxford house.

Right: Panels of Venetian glass filter red light into the front hallway of the Falkner-Gary House.

was no such thing as central heating during the early years of our residence in Oxford. Each room in the house, except the kitchen, had a fireplace. In cold weather . . . fires would be made up in the grates of the bedrooms. How pleasant it was on such nights to lie in bed, after the light had been extinguished, with the quilts pulled up snugly beneath the chin, listening to the cold rain against the windowpanes, the warm and caressing glow of the fireplace reaching up and out as it enveloped the whole room from floor to ceiling."[52]

In 1905, Murry Falkner moved his family a few blocks away to South Street (now South Lamar Avenue.) Their old house was sold to Johnny Brown, later to Kate Baker, and at some point the back hallway was converted into a dining room and the original kitchen converted to a bedroom. The flue opening for the wood stove is still visible in that bedroom.

As often happened with Gothic-style houses, its unusual lines fell out of favor and the house was abandoned in midcentury. Wild ghost stories and tall tales grew up along with the weeds and vines of the vast yard, and generations of Oxford children dared each other to approach the dilapidated home. When Knox and Betty Gary discovered it in the 1970s, the windows were broken out and dust covered every interior surface. They took on the task of restoring not only the main house but also Mammy Callie's cabin in the rear, and both structures stand now as Oxford treasures, carefully refurbished and full of life.

Empty and decaying for years, the Falkner-Gary House was saved by Knox and Betty Gary in the 1970s.

MADISON COUNTY COURTHOUSE

MISSISSIPPI IS DIVIDED into eighty-two counties, each with at least one courthouse. Ten of those counties, for reasons that have often been forgotten over the years, have two county seats and two courthouses. They range from mundane, unremarkable structures that could just as easily house a hardware store or a factory to those that practically shout local pride. Some are small but elaborate, others massive but gawky and architecturally unappealing. Many occupy the quintessential "square," surrounded by downtown businesses and offices, the result of the town's designation as a county seat before the courthouse was built. Classic examples with this arrangement are Holly Springs, Oxford, and Woodville. Towns that developed before their choice as the government center may have the building off on a side lot, as in Senatobia and Greenwood.

One of the most photographed and famous courthouses in Mississippi is the 1857 Greek Revival Madison County Courthouse in Canton. Its stunning symmetry and pristine detailing, along with its classic "Old South" square

of banks, drugstores, lawyers' offices, and dime stores has earned it a place in several movies and in the hearts of generations of Madison Countians.

The county grew out of Indian lands ceded in the 1820 Treaty of Doak's Stand. Had there been a viable, water-navigable site in the region, the state capital would likely have been located there, near the geographic center of the new state. But the men assigned the task of finding a place to put that capital city didn't care for the terrain along the Big Black River and wound up recommending LeFleur's Bluff, some twenty miles south on the Pearl River.

When Madison County was formed, its county seat moved around, from tiny Beatty's Bluff to Livingston, Madisonville, and then to the site that would be Canton. Killis and Margaret Walton deeded forty acres of their farm over for the location of the new town, and the courthouse square was laid out with a central green and four encircling streets for businesses and offices. By the time the first crude frame court building was replaced with a more permanent structure in 1838, the town had pulled in over four hundred citizens. It boasted a jail, several churches, a girls' school, two banks, two hotels, ten dry goods stores, two watchmakers, and a wealth of hungry lawyers. Dunbar Rowland, Mississippi's first state archivist, described the young town as "seem[ing] to have been more litigious than diseased at this early period, with sixteen attorneys and only six physicians."[53]

By 1850, the second courthouse had been declared unsafe, and plans were being laid for a new one. Madison County, like many of its neighbors, was enjoying the prosperity of a booming antebellum cotton economy. The citizens of Canton and the surrounding area wanted their new courthouse to mirror that success, and for that purpose they hired one of the South's premier architects, Joseph Willis. Willis had designed the Jackson City Hall, the Rankin County Courthouse at Brandon, and other public buildings around the South. He was paid four hundred dollars for his design and contracting work on the Canton courthouse, and the results of his talent are evident today.

Finished at a total cost of little more than twenty-six thousand dollars, the courthouse is a solid brick cube, highlighted with Doric columns, engaged pilasters, a full classical frieze, and triglyphs. Topping the low-pitched roof is a domed tower, the subject of much controversy as the building was nearing completion. As the formal acceptance date of January 6, 1858, approached, and with one session of circuit court having already been held in the nearly finished structure, E. Moody was hired to take the dome off. Rumors were rampant that the tower was too heavy and unsafe for those inside the building. Newspaper editors warned their readers to steer clear of the courthouse.

> From what we have heard about this building, the dome is too heavy for the roof to support. Hence it is shaken about by the wind, and the roof is so injured as to be subject to constant leak. Unless some plan be devised for supporting the dome by other means than the roof, there will always be leaking after every wind of more than ordinary violence. To accomplish this end is the business of the architect who undertook this work, and nothing less than this will satisfy the people of this County. The contractor may, from time to time, by the application of putty or other similar expedients, temporarily stop leaks; but the next wind will cause his wounds to bleed afresh. We venture the opinion that the Court House will never be in condition to be used, until the dome is supported by suitable columns, so as to prevent its agitation by the wind.[54]

The women of Canton, who apparently found the dome a charming touch, kicked up such a fuss that the newspaper and other detractors capitulated and let the building stand as it was. Willis soon moved on to a successful career in Memphis, far from the meddling sidewalk architects in Canton. His courthouse, dome and all, has survived war, tornadoes, an 1869 fire that devastated the

One of the most celebrated Greek Revival structures in Mississippi, the Madison County Courthouse was dedicated in 1857.

east side of the square, and almost a century and a half of wear and tear. It has housed dramatic trials and more than one murder in its halls and on its lawn. Justice was often swift. After G. P. Kemp gunned down J. G. Thigpen on the courthouse grounds in 1881, he found himself in the courtroom on trial that night and headed down the steps after his acquittal the following morning.

The Madison County Courthouse has undergone several renovations, the most recent in the mid-1990s. It has become internationally famous, not only through movie exposure, but as the centerpiece of the semiannual Canton Flea Market, an arts and crafts festival which draws tens of thousands of visitors each April and October.

CHRIST EPISCOPAL CHURCH

IN ONE OF THE MOST isolated and largely forgotten corners of Mississippi, abandoned by the river and never discovered by the major highways, the rural community of Church Hill holds only a few plantation manors, the last remnants of what was once a prosperous and thriving frontier town. Other than the houses, only a decrepit country store and one remarkable building bear witness to a vanished settlement.

Church Hill takes its name from an architectural gem, a tiny Gothic chapel so true to its medieval English roots that it seems to have been transported through time and space to this Jefferson County knoll. Rectangular in form, with a gabled roof and rose window, Christ Church reflects its Gothic forebears with its buttresses and simulated ashlar masonry. The interior is graced with a rare hammerbeam ceiling, grained to resemble oak. A semioctagonal lectern is matched with a carved pulpit. Even the original pipe organ remains, though it has long been inoperable.

The Episcopal Church took root early in Mississippi, but not without its struggles. The Mississippi Territory attracted religious proselytizers of every stripe, some with official church sanction and others driven by a divine inspiration to bring their personal gospel to this wild and undisciplined land. One of the first to appear was Adam Cloud, a Delaware native who may or may not have been ordained in the Episcopal Church of his home state. He settled in Natchez during the height of Spanish rule and began to preach, upsetting the Catholic hierarchy. The Spanish overseers had no quarrel with Protestant preachers, so long as they kept a low profile. Cloud angered them so much with his public proclamations that Governor Gayoso had him sent off to New Orleans in chains.

As soon as the Spanish flag was lowered over Natchez in 1798, Reverend Cloud was back. With his small congregation following, he established a church in the Cole's Creek area north of Natchez, meeting in a crude log structure. Over the next thirty years, this seminal church would grow and become Christ Episcopal Church. By 1829, they

had pulled together three thousand dollars and erected a more suitable chapel on a slight rise. Tennessee bishop James H. Otey rode through in 1838 and was pleased with what he found: "We rode to Christ's Church—a plain, brick edifice—this morning, and found a congregation respectable in number and appearance awaiting our coming—the whole seemed devout and attentive—The people of this neighborhood, I learn, are very favorably disposed to the Church. Several planters with their families are decidedly attached to our ecclesiastical order and worship upon principle, and they are willing to contribute liberally and cheerfully for the support of the institutions of the Gospel. I have seldom, if ever, seen a country parish in which a minister can be so pleasantly situated, and with the same prospect of usefulness."[55]

Left: Christ Episcopal Church traces its roots back to territorial preacher Adam Cloud.

Right: Christ Church was consecrated in June 1858, and its graveyard includes members born before Mississippi's statehood.

With support from wealthy plantation owners, the scions of mansions like the Cedars, Richland, and Oak Grove, Christ Church continued to prosper and expand. By 1856, vestry minutes were reflecting the desire of the congregation for a new building, which would meet "the wants and tastes of a country congregation, consulting to comfort and convenience before architectural elegance and beauty."[56] Natchez lawyer J. Edward Smith, who seemed to be more prolific at architecture than law, designed the new church, and Nathaniel Loomis Carpenter served as his contractor. The plaster work was performed by Robert Scudamore. The hammer-beam ceiling was grained by at least three proud workmen, who signed and dated their effort on May 17, 1858.

The fine new church was consecrated in June 1858 by Bishop William Mercer Green. Bishop Green was familiar with several other Gothic chapels around the state, but he found Church Hill's location and ambience to be particularly gratifying. "On approaching the site of the old Church, I was pleased to find in its stead a structure not only more commodious and Church-like, but more tasteful in style, and becoming in all adornment."[57]

As with two other churches which he had consecrated, St. John's of Glen Allan and Chapel of the Cross in Madison, Bishop Green's comments would reflect the last active and peaceful days of Christ Church. Although this corner of Mississippi was spared significant battles during the Civil War, roaming bands of Union troops found their way to Church Hill in 1864. Whether from boredom, resentment, or sheer malice, they forced their way into the church and left the members offended if not harmed. "[In] 1864 it was entered by a band of Yankee ruffians, belonging to an Illinois regiment stationed at Natchez, who danced in the chancel, played lewd airs on the organ and wound up their sacrilege by stealing a part of the silver plate composing the Communion Service."[58]

After repeated blows from war, economic depression, and the declining population of Church Hill, Christ Church suffered. Many of the wealthy patrons died or moved away from the increasingly isolated county, taking their patronage with them. The dedication of the few remaining members and helpful sister congregations has allowed the church to survive, and services are still held once a month. The communion silver service still bears the scars inflicted by Union soldiers, and one collection plate has a sword slash on the bottom side.

Christ Church remains one of the most visually stunning sights in Mississippi, a totally unexpected jewel hovering above a sharp curve on the old road from Port Gibson to Natchez.

VICKSBURG'S OLD COURTHOUSE MUSEUM

WHEN REVEREND NEWIT VICK laid out plans for a city on the bluffs of Walnut Hills, he reserved a number of lots for himself and his extended family. The most desirable lot was obvious even in its undeveloped state, a graceful hill that soared high above the Mississippi River just a stone's throw from the water's edge.

Vick died of yellow fever within days of the sale of Vicksburg's first lot. His son-in-law, John Lane, would see to the actual development of the town, including a provision stipulating that the prime hillside lot must always be reserved for public use. When Vicksburg's wharves attracted hundreds of steamboats and it developed into Mississippi's most economically diverse antebellum community, it replaced Warrenton as the county seat. The obvious place for a new courthouse was on Newit Vick's hill.

That courthouse burned in April 1857. Flush with their reputation as the premier river city of the 1850s, the townspeople voted for a tax that would cover the seventy-five-thousand-dollar cost of a new Warren County Courthouse. Appropriately for its location, it would be far and away the grandest and largest in the state. Designed by the Weldon brothers of Natchez, the courthouse was to be a towering two-story Greek Revival structure with Ionic columns and porticoes on each façade. The construction was overseen by a Weldon slave, John Jackson, who supervised the production and laying of thousands of bricks. These were mortared together with a sugar-based mixture and then plastered over with cement. Baker Iron Company of Cincinnati cast huge Ionic capitals, shutters and interior stairways, which were shipped down the Ohio and Mississippi rivers to Vicksburg.

After more than a year of labor, the new courthouse was finally complete. The combination of its sheer size, its monumental bell tower, and its location on the city's highest point made it altogether imposing. Little did the hundreds who turned out for the dedication realize that within a few years, this building would become a nationally recognized symbol of southern resistance and defeat.

Warren County sent moderate representatives to the Secession Convention in Jackson. The town had little to gain and much to lose from war, but its spokesmen were outnumbered and finally signed the Ordinance of Secession in January 1861. Within weeks, eager troops were parading their new uniforms and drilling on the courthouse grounds, never dreaming that the war they were so excited about would come to a fateful climax in their own backyard.

By late 1862, control of the Mississippi River had become Ulysses Grant's obsession. He couldn't slip his gunboats past it from the north or the south, and a back-door feint through the Mississippi Delta proved a dismal failure. Plans to dig a canal through Louisiana and divert the river away from Vicksburg were quickly shelved. General Grant finally hit upon the solution to Vicksburg: march his troops through the Louisiana backwoods until they were south of Vicksburg, then cross the Mississippi at Bruinsburg and march up through the state.

Grant succeeded in ferrying his men across the river and fought a series of battles at Port Gibson, Raymond, Jackson, Champion Hill, and the Big Black River. They arrived on the eastern outskirts of Vicksburg in mid-May 1863, and laid down siege lines. Nine miles of fortifications and trenches were filled with Confederate soldiers under the command of General John C. Pemberton. The river was blocked in both directions by Union gunboats. With Vicksburg cut off from the outside world, the siege was on.

From the outset of hostilities in Vicksburg, the courthouse was a highly visible and desirable target. Before the forty-seven-day siege plunged townspeople into a nightmare of constant shelling and deprivation, Mary Loughborough and her friends lightheartedly climbed the courthouse stairs for a better view of the developing tension. "Some of our friends proposed going for a better view up on the balcony around the cupola of the court house. The view from there was most extensive and beautiful. Hill after hill arose in the distance, enclosing the city in the form of a crescent. Immediately in the center . . . the firing seemed more continuous, while to the left and running northerly, the rattle and roar would be sudden, sharp and vigorous, then ceasing for some time."[59]

Once the Union gunboats lined up on the river, casual gazing from the courthouse balcony was no longer so much fun. Shells were lobbed at the inviting target, and one actually nicked a corner of the west portico. Word was sent to the boats that Union prisoners were being held in the building, and the shelling came to an abrupt halt. This ruse probably saved the courthouse from destruction.

After a long, horrifying seven weeks, General Pemberton surrendered the city on July 4, 1863. Gettysburg's battle was decided the same day, but many military historians consider the loss of Vicksburg more damning to the Confederacy, as it gave total control of the Mississippi River to the North.

Jubilant Union soldiers paraded through the streets of the conquered city and up the terraces to the courthouse. Two officers of an Ohio cavalry unit clambered up the clock tower and lowered the Confederate flag, replacing it with an American banner. As the soldiers swarmed through the building, one stopped to stare at the elabo-

Vicksburg's Old Courthouse Museum survived Civil War shelling and abandonment by the county to become one of the state's most eclectic museums.

rate iron staircase, stamped with the words "Baker Iron Company, Cincinnati, Ohio." He noted wryly that a people who couldn't even produce their own staircases didn't stand much chance of winning a war.

Considering that it suffered more during the Civil War than any other Mississippi town, Vicksburg recovered remarkably quickly. Caves where whole families had cowered and prayed for their lives were abandoned. The wharves on the river reopened and rail service was restored. Centered among some of the state's richest agricultural land and blessed with easy access to water, Vicksburg regained its economic standing and even lobbied to become Mississippi's new capital city. Jackson's capitol building was in increasingly decrepit condition and the town was struggling to put its "Chimneyville" reputation behind it. Warren County supervisors, sensing an opening, launched a campaign to declare Vicksburg the new state capital and move the government into the big courthouse on the hill. Nothing ever came of the offer, but it served to show the pride local people felt in this symbolic survivor of dark days.

In the late 1800s and early 1900s, veterans of both sides of the Civil War flocked to Vicksburg to remember the exploits of their youth. They would join local families on the courthouse terraces for weekend concerts and picnics. Out of their interest and the efforts of patriotic clubs grew the Vicksburg National Military Park Association and, eventually, the park itself.

With time, all public buildings tend to have a period of declining significance and utility, and the Warren County Courthouse was no exception. When a shining art deco courthouse facility was completed in the 1930s, the supervisors began making plans to sell off the prime real estate where the eighty-year-old courthouse sat. Fortunately, someone dug up John Lane's deed reserving the property for public use in perpetuity. Since there was no profit to be made off the aging courthouse, the supervisors simply locked the door and ignored it.

Neglect took its toll on the courthouse over the next few years. If not for the efforts of Eva Davis, a determined and resourceful woman who loved the decrepit old structure, it likely would have caved in on itself and been lost forever. Mrs. Davis cajoled a key from the supervisors and spent months hauling buckets of water up the steep hill from the street. In the dark halls and courtrooms of the electricity-stripped courthouse, she scrubbed floors and worked through mountains of paperwork and trash. Gradually, inspired by her example, other volunteers joined her. From their efforts, the Vicksburg and Warren County Historical Society was born, and people cleaned their attics out to stock a museum in the courthouse. It remains one of Mississippi's most eclectic and interesting collections, and the building is now officially the Old Courthouse–Eva Whitaker Davis Memorial.

WINDSOR

A NARROW, TWISTING ROAD leads from Port Gibson to Lorman, its isolation intensified by the deep gullies that peel away from the asphalt and slow the most foolhardy driver. Kudzu creeps toward the road from every direction, and wisteria vines and dogwoods burst out of the green landscape that seems to rise up and encapsulate this part of Mississippi.

It takes a sharp eye to spot the small brown sign pointing to Windsor. Nothing suggests that this site is anything more than another barren field or run-of-the-mill old house. But at the end of the gravel drive, just beyond tangled underbrush and scrub oaks, stand twenty-eight columns, at once grand and tragic, rising like an ancient ruined temple in the midst of a Mississippi forest.

Those columns and assorted piles of crumbled bricks and melted iron are all that remain of the grandest of all the state's antebellum mansions. Windsor was the culmination of a fifty-year

game of one-upmanship, played with stone and mortar and vast wealth by cotton planters and money men, each determined to outdo his neighbor or his brother. From the time the first mansions, houses like Concord and Gloucester and Auburn, rose in Natchez, to the late 1850s, when Longwood, Waverley, and Stanton Hall raised the stakes to unimaginable heights, the architectural warfare in Mississippi was waged with wild abandon.

Windsor was the dream house of Smith Coffee Daniell II. Unlike many of the other fabulously wealthy planters of the day, Daniell was a native Mississippian. He was heir to several vast plantations in his own state and Louisiana, and his marriage to a distant cousin increased his acreage to an estimated twenty thousand acres. By the mid-1850s, he had chosen the spot for a mansion that would far outshine even the finest of Natchez or Vicksburg. He would build it near Bruinsburg, a tiny river town just south of Port Gibson. Slaves would do the bulk

of the brick work, but northern artisans would be brought in for detail plastering, ironwork, and specialty touches.

Work on Windsor began in 1859. For two years, a brick kiln fired thousands of sixteen-inch-long bricks and triangular molds for the columns. Wagons were sent to Bruinsburg to carry back the massive iron capitals, balustrades, and staircases, all wrought in St. Louis and shipped south to Mississippi by steamboat. Gradually, the raised basement level was completed and the two main floors were fashioned. Twenty-nine Corinthian columns outlined the L-shaped house plan.

When the workmen finally put away their tools, the house they surveyed contained twenty-three huge rooms and soared to a fourth-floor cupola. The main block featured a basement that was actually a functional city in itself. Rooms were assigned for a dairy, a commissary, schoolroom, and doctor's office. On the main level, reached by the elegant iron stairways, was a broad central hallway with a spiral stair, three formal rooms, and a bedroom suite. The suite included a bathroom, a true rarity of the day.

Upstairs were more bedrooms and another bath. In the rear ell were the kitchen, dining room, and still more bedrooms. Topping it all was a square cupola, glazed with clear panes and decorated with corner columns. Just beneath it,

the attic held innovative tanks, eight feet by twenty feet and five feet deep. Rainwater was diverted from the roof into the tanks and then funneled into the bathrooms on the two main levels.

The details of the interior were as fine as the overall scheme for Windsor. Georgia and Tennessee marble outlined the numerous fireplaces, and chandeliers were reflected in floor-to-ceiling mirrors throughout the formal rooms. Total cost for the house and its furnishings was estimated at over $175,000, a phenomenal sum for 1860.

Smith Daniell may have been blessed with ambition and riches above and beyond his peers, but his timing was abysmal. As the finishing touches were placed on Windsor, war was stirring in Charleston Harbor. And within a few weeks of moving his family into the mansion, Daniell himself was dead at the age of thirty-four. His widow, Catherine, took over the day-to-day operations of the huge house, with ample assistance from a small army of slaves. She had no idea that within two years the war that was just starting in far-off Virginia would land on the very doorstep of her great house.

Page 115: The solid-iron capitals for Windsor's Corinthian columns were manufactured in St. Louis, shipped downriver to Bruinsburg, and carried by wagon to the building site.

Left: The columns of Windsor are all that remain of Smith Daniell's massive twenty-three-room mansion.

Right: A century and a half of weather and wear has peeled much of the stucco from Windsor's column bases, revealing the intricate brickwork underneath.

General Ulysses Grant had been stymied in every approach to Vicksburg, the last Confederate stronghold on the Mississippi River. In the spring of 1863, he marched tens of thousands of Federal troops through Louisiana and ferried them across the river at Bruinsburg. Their goal was Vicksburg, but they would approach it by a circuitous route that would result in battles at Port Gibson, Raymond, and Champion Hill. Their trek took them right by the gates of Windsor, where a young Ohio lieutenant pulled out his sketchbook and left us the only existing eyewitness drawing of the home he labeled "House near Bruinsburg, Mississippi."

Windsor survived the war and use as a hospital after the Battle of Port Gibson. The Daniell children grew up there, and it became the logical social center of Claiborne County. It was a careless guest at one of the parties who brought down Smith Daniell's dream in 1890. "The palatial dwelling on Windsor plantation, near Bethel Church in southwestern part of the county, burned to the ground last Monday. The fire, of which the origin is unknown, was discovered about noon, but it could not be checked, and in a few hours this splendid country site was in ruins. Most of the contents were also destroyed. These included not only a great deal of elegant furniture, but many costly heirlooms and other household property of value, such as jewelry, silver plate, a large library, etc. . . . We regret to learn that neither upon it nor its contents was there any insurance."[60]

All known photographs of the mansion were lost in the fire, as were the original house plans. Until the Union soldier's diary was discovered in the Ohio State Archives a century later, only the memories of those fortunate enough to have lived in or visited Windsor preserved the details of the unparalleled magnificence. Smith C. Daniell IV was a child when the house burned, but its loss left a lasting impression on him: "On Monday, February 17, 1890, while a house party was being enjoyed by the young people, neighbors and friends, about 10:30 a.m., they went up to the observatory, including myself, to get a good view of the river and Louisiana. Coming down, a young man threw his cigarette into some trash made by carpenters doing some repairs on Saturday . . . I stopped in the hall on the third floor to play on a piano I called my own. Emily Williams, a house girl, hollered 'Fire!' Two buckets of water were sent up, but it was too late, and I was told to leave the house."[61]

By afternoon, Windsor was a smoldering pile. The interior was totally gutted, and the furnishings, chandeliers, and marble mantels lay twisted in unidentifiable heaps of ash-covered ruin. One set of iron steps was salvaged and carried down to Alcorn A & M College, where it was attached to Jeremiah Chamberlain's chapel, along with a few sections of balustrade. The Daniell family rebuilt elsewhere, and the site of Windsor was gradually taken over by live oaks and moss. When strong spring winds blew across the Mississippi River, columns would topple and fall, their huge iron capitals imbedding themselves in the dust.

Remarkably, most of the columns never fell. WPA photos from the mid-1930s show them still outlining the ghostly remains of Windsor, with trees and bushes sprouting from the tops of the rusty capitals. In 1974, the descendants of the Daniell family deeded the property to the Mississippi Department of Archives and History, which has maintained the site since. Of the columns still standing, some look almost new and others are merely stubs, their stucco peeled away and the crumbling bricks peeking through. In their decay, they remain an instantly recognizable symbol of the Old South and the long-lost heyday of Mississippi's antebellum culture.

PROVINE CHAPEL

In antebellum Mississippi, education was an uncertain and often nonexistent promise. Governor after governor and legislature after legislature pledged funding and support for schools and colleges, all to no avail, and decades passed with no realization of those claims. Territorial governor W. C. C. Claiborne urged the opening of a "seminary of learning"; two decades later, Governor George Poindexter lamented that "[t]here is scarcely a seminary of learning among us worthy of the name; perhaps not one. The rudiments of the English language are taught in a few private schools dispersed over a wide extent of the country, and even there met with poor encouragement, and are often conducted by incompetent teachers."[62]

Attempts were made, primarily by private individuals or churches, to provide some sort of basic education for Mississippi's young people. Most were minimally staffed, poorly funded and short-lived. Of the numerous "academies" and "institutions" which sprang up in Mississippi's earliest years, very few survived more than a term or two and only three still exist in some form.

Hampstead Academy grew out of disappointment. Mt. Salus, a burgeoning Natchez Trace community just west of Jackson, lobbied the legislature for designation as the state's capital city when Jackson foundered. By one vote, the town that would become Clinton lost out. Tempers flared, duels were fought, and the more practical citizens chose to promote their town as an academic center. Hampstead Academy opened in 1826 with broad local support. With rumors swirling that the legislature might finally designate a state university, hopeful Clintonians changed the name of their school to Mississippi Academy.

Their enthusiasm was premature. Not until 1841 would the legislature finally establish a formal public university and choose Oxford as the site. Support for Mississippi Academy waned, and it would have disappeared like so many other schools if the Presbyterian Church had not stepped up and purchased the charter. They controlled it until 1850, at which point it was sold to the Baptist Church. The name was changed once again, and the school has been known as Mississippi College ever since.

Along with its sister school, Central Female Institute (later Hillman College), Mississippi College grew at an impressive clip throughout the 1850s. Perhaps seeking to maintain its image after the new state university in Oxford completed its grand Lyceum, the Mississippi Baptist Convention established a one-hundred-thousand-dollar endowment fund to erect a central chapel building on the Clinton campus. Plans were drawn up by noted architect Jacob Larmour, the man responsible for such triumphs as Grace Episcopal Church in Canton and Annandale in Madison.

Larmour's plans called for a Greek Revival temple-form building on a massive scale. Three stories tall, with monumental Corinthian columns and windows, it dwarfed all other buildings on the Mississippi College campus. The chapel stretched 110 feet from front to rear and 56 feet across the façade. A raised basement housed functional rooms, while the main floor contained a sanctuary with cypress and walnut pews, kerosene-fired chandeliers and two-feet-thick exterior walls.

Larmour began building the chapel in early 1859. By May 1860, it was ready for commencement services. That gala occasion would be the only one observed for several years. The following spring, the Mississippi College Rifles were mustered into Confederate service in the sanctuary. The school stayed open but awarded only two degrees in 1862. All but one member of the faculty resigned, leaving only Professor I. N. Urner to piddle around the empty campus, teaching anyone who might show up and protecting the property.

Most of the students were fighting elsewhere when war reached Clinton. Alice Shirley Eaton, a student at nearby Central Female Institute, remembered the 1863 scene: "The usually quiet village of Clinton was now all confusion. The soldiers were bent on destruction, stables were torn down, smoke houses invaded and emptied of their bacon and hams, chicken houses were depopulated, vehicles of all kinds were taken or destroyed, barrels of sugar and molasses . . . were emptied, the molasses running in streams in the yard . . . The bees, not liking to be dis-

Left: Only one graduation ceremony was held in Provine Chapel before the Civil War took most of Mississippi College's student body.

Right: Provine Chapel, the dominant element of Mississippi College's quadrangle, is fronted by Dr. Sam Gore's sculpture of Christ and his disciples.

turbed, and attracted also by the flowing molasses, hovered around in large numbers and directed much of their attention to the soldiers, adding still more to the confusion."[63]

Mississippi College and the chapel were in the midst of the turmoil. The empty sanctuary was commandeered for Union troops and the basement turned into a stable. College legend tells of a black caretaker who snuffed out the fires started by departing Federal soldiers. The battle moved on to Vicksburg, and Clintonians breathed a sigh of relief.

The school reopened soon after the war, unlike most other antebellum academies and quasi-colleges. The campus expanded around the main building, which gradually took on the affectionate title of Old Chapel. Clinton's First Baptist Church shared the space with Mississippi College, providing a preacher on the first and third Sundays, relieved by a professor on the second, fourth, and fifth Sabbaths. When First Baptist built its own sanctuary across College Street in 1922, Old Chapel reverted to its academic roots.

By World War II, the college had absorbed Hillman College and outgrown the Old Chapel sanctuary. Nelson Hall was under construction, with a spacious new auditorium, classroom, and administrative space. After its completion, fewer and fewer functions found their way to the Old Chapel. The building was caving in to the inevitable stress of a century's wear, and serious consideration was given to tearing it down. In 1960, with alumni increasingly unhappy about the impending loss of the campus's only antebellum building, the board of trustees voted to renovate and restore Old Chapel. A $140,000 project refurbished the sanctuary and converted the basement into classrooms and offices.

In 1969, Old Chapel was officially renamed Provine Chapel, in honor of the longtime Mississippi College president J. W. Provine. The campus has continued to expand and adapt with the times, but the chapel is unchanged, the proud symbol of the state's oldest university.

FIRST PRESBYTERIAN CHURCH OF PORT GIBSON

REVEREND ZEBULON BUTLER was an ecclesiastical legend in Claiborne County and southwest Mississippi, famous for his fiery sermons and dramatic flourishes. His congregation came to expect fire and brimstone homilies, which were often punctuated with the preacher's uplifted fist, index finger jabbing toward the heavens as he hammered home a warning to the wayward. That gesture was, by local legend, immortalized in the huge golden hand which crowns the steeple of the First Presbyterian Church in Port Gibson. Reverend Butler was the guiding force behind the formation and construction of that church, and his own funeral was the first service performed there.

The Synod of Carolina sent three intrepid ministers to the wilds of the Mississippi Territory in 1800. One of the churches they organized was Bayou Pierre Presbyterian, just south of the fledgling town of Port Gibson. As the community grew, the church relocated for the convenience of its members, and the First Presbyterian Church of Port Gibson was officially incorporated on the first day of January 1827.

Zebulon Butler had traveled to Mississippi from Wilkes Barre, Pennsylvania, intent on starting a church in Vicksburg. That river town, with its gamblers and fast style, was not especially interested in having a stern Presbyterian riding herd on its morals. One of Butler's Princeton classmates, Allison Ross, was living in Port Gibson and heard that Butler was on the lookout for a congregation. He convinced fifty of his fellow Presbyterians to put together a generous offer for Butler, who was headed for Bethel Church, near Lorman. "He was halted and a letter placed in his hands; its purpose was to inform him that $300 was deposited in the bank for him, and a subscription of $12,000 was raised, and the citizens of Port Gibson desired him to preach the gospel to them; if the salary was not

sufficient, he was requested to name the amount. If a voice had called audibly from heaven, he would not have been more profoundly amazed!"[64]

Reverend Butler knew a good deal when he saw it. He accepted the church's offer and led it in its first building program. The small brick sanctuary housed the congregation until the preacher's popularity had swelled their number to more than 150 souls. An ambitious plan was laid to build an unusually large brick and stone church, one that would far outshine the neighboring Methodists, Baptists, and Episcopalians.

James Jones was hired to design the new church. Combining elements of Gothic Revival and Romanesque Revival, Jones's building would consist primarily of a spacious sanctuary, measuring sixty-six feet in length and forty-nine feet wide. The wooden curved ceiling soared thirty-six feet above the pulpit, geometrically balanced to project the preacher's voice from the choir to the last pew without artificial amplification.

Word of impending war led Jones to return to his home outside of the South with only the walls of the church completed. Elder H. N. Spencer took over supervision, contributing eight thousand dollars of his own funds to see the project through to completion. He may have hired

Page 123: Daniel Foley carved the original heaven-pointing hand of wood; the 1890 metal replacement is covered with gold leaf.

Left: Port Gibson's First Presbyterian Church was constructed under the leadership of Reverend Zebulon Butler, whose funeral was the first to be held in its sanctuary.

Right: The 1903 stained-glass windows of Port Gibson's First Presbyterian Church are hinged to allow air circulation.

William English, a talented plaster artisan who carved beautiful molding around the windows and doorways and supported the slave balcony with heavy scrolled brackets. The arched windows on the front façade were glazed in multicolored diamond panes, oriented to cast rainbows of light into the vestibule.

As elaborate as the interior of the church was, its most notable feature was, and remains, the golden hand atop the steeple. The original was wooden, carved by Daniel Foley, who was likely just a teenager at the time. From the base of the hand's wrist to the end of the carefully manicured index finger was a full fourteen feet. The other three fingers and thumb were clenched in Zebulon Butler's characteristic fist.

Reverend Butler may not have lived to see the hand rise above his church. Just a week after the formal dedication ceremonies were conducted by Oakland College president W. L. Breckinridge, Zebulon Butler died. A month later, Port Gibson and Mississippi would leave the Union. Economic distress followed, leaving the congregation's account exhausted. There was no money left to buy interior furnishings and benches, so the pews were auctioned off to individual families. Many have been handed down through multiple generations to the present day.

The Presbyterian Church survived the Battle of Port Gibson and the march of Ulysses Grant's troops down the main street of the town. Realizing that they occupied a truly unique house of worship, the congregation took great pains to maintain and improve its condition. A one-ton bell was installed in the tower, and the town helped pay for the clock mechanism. New stained-glass windows, ingeniously hinged to allow passage of air into the sanctuary, were installed in 1903. Mr. and Mrs. William Parker, owners of the famed steamboat *Robert E. Lee*, donated kerosene-burning chandeliers from the boat.

By 1890, the giant hand was riddled with woodpecker holes, presenting a hollow, unstable hazard to townspeople and visitors who came to marvel at the sight. It was pulled down and replaced with an exact metal replica, covered in gold leaf. Its last trip to the ground was in 1989, when it was repaired and replated with .0003-inch-thick German-manufactured gold leaf. Church members lined up to have their photos made by the hand, celebrating its ascension to another century above their most unique sanctuary.

VICTORIA

ABERDEEN IS A TOWN which was fortunate enough to know prosperity in the antebellum years and again in the late 1800s. As a result, its streets are lined with Greek Revival mansions, Gothic showplaces, and one of the most extensive collections of Victorian cottages in Mississippi. The most elegant of these latter houses are scattered along Franklin Street, more commonly known as Silk Stocking Row. Their vibrant colors and profusion of gables, carved woodwork, and fanciful windows make this a unique architectural treasure found nowhere else in the state.

Standing on the west side of Franklin Street is Victoria, a bright blue frame house with a history that often belied the charm of its façade. Sharply pointed twin gables frame a covered porch, with flattened arch scrollwork connecting the carved columns. No less than seven types of siding represent the gamut of 1870s woodwork: shingle, clapboard, board-and-batten, diagonal beading, scrollwork panels, reversed board-and-batten, and reversed clapboard. The main entrance is highlighted with original red Venetian glass panes, and each of the main rooms inside has a fixed transom of varying colored glass.

Victoria was built around 1870 in Colonel John Hampton's back garden. Colonel Hampton designed it for his daughter, Unity, as a wedding present. Something went awry, the wedding was cancelled, and Unity may never have lived in the cottage at all. It wound up in the hands of a cousin, Ophelia Hampton, known to generations of Aberdonians as "Miss Phe."

Miss Phe never married. In the early 1900s, she took in her niece, Gertrude Bumpass, who had been blinded at a young age by an optic nerve tumor. Gertrude lived on in Victoria after her aunt's death, cared for by an increasingly unkempt parade of caretakers and boarders. They didn't care about the house and Gertrude couldn't see what was happening, even if she did care. The house sagged and accumulated dirt and grime like a magnet. Floors caved in, curtains hardened with layers of dust, and grit and chimneys crumbled.

When Gertrude passed away in the mid-1970s, her will directed nonexistent funds to numerous causes. The house was left to a distant relative who was totally unaware of its existence and not at all pleased with the prospect of restoring the decrepit old place. It seemed doomed until local banker Jim Crosby, involved in the settling of the estate, saw the potential in it. Beyond the decades of filth were the original walls, hardwood floors, fourteen-foot ceilings, and a century of Aberdeen history.

In a stroke of good fortune for Mississippi history buffs, Mr. Crosby took on Victoria and has spent thirty years restoring it, doing most of the work by hand. A variety of unique and unusual antiques are found in each room, including a cannonball bed whose headboard had been used as an attic stair and bookcases salvaged from Aberdeen's first drugstore.

After generations of neglect and decay, Victoria is now a proud part of Silk Stocking Row. It survives as a rare example of fine building techniques prominent in the first years following the Civil War.

Left: Victoria is one of the most elaborate homes on Aberdeen's Silk Stocking Row, a street renowned for its late nineteenth-century architecture.

Above left: Fanciful chimney stacks and seven types of siding are found on the exterior of Victoria.

Above right: A tragic tale of elderly spinsters, surprised heirs, and an undaunted banker is part of Victoria's legacy.

TATE COUNTY COURTHOUSE

DeSoto County once stretched from the Mississippi-Tennessee line, just below Memphis, all the way down to Panola County. Government business was transacted in the castle-like Hernando courthouse, the fanciful creation of Felix LaBauve. But folks in the southern part of the county were forced to ferry or ride across the appropriately named Coldwater River, resulting in innumerable accidents and drownings.

The state legislature solved the Coldwater River dilemma with the creation of Tate County in 1873. Pulling land from DeSoto, Tunica, and Marshall counties, they named it for local landowner Simpson Tate. There was only one town of any size in the new county, so tiny Senatobia would be the county seat by default.

Courthouse squares are a product of towns that are created for the express purpose of serving as the county seat. When a new county is formed with existing communities, the courthouse has to be shoehorned in wherever it will fit. Such was the case in Senatobia, where the Tate County Courthouse was built on a side street, several blocks from the heart of downtown. So it's all the more startling, when driving through Senatobia, to see the Italianate/Romanesque Revival tower peeking above the rooftops of store buildings, and even more surprising to find such a dramatic and elegant structure tucked away on a shady lot off the main thoroughfare.

After Tate County was created, designs for the proposed courthouse were submitted by several firms. The chosen plan was drawn up by James B. Cook of Memphis. Cook was one of the Reconstruction South's most revered architects, with a long and colorful pedigree. Born in England, he trained at King's College and was commissioned to build the Victoria and Albert Bridge over the Thames and the Crystal Palace Exhibit in Hyde Park. After moving to Memphis, he was responsible for the first

The architect of the Tate County Courthouse was responsible for the Crystal Palace, a pyramid, and a revered hotel before he worked in Senatobia.

Gayoso Hotel and the 1897 Tennessee Centennial's Temple of Cheops Pyramid.

Cook was obviously a man of exuberant imagination. He pulled out all the stops with his Tate County commission, giving Senatobia one of the most notable courthouses in all of Mississippi or the South. Calvert Vaux's 1864 plan book, *Villas and Cottages*, provided the rough outline of the building. Cook adapted it into an H-shaped two-story masonry structure with a four-story bell tower. Engaged buttresses on the north and south façades are optically designed to simulate tapering. Windows are semicircular arches with corbelled hoods. The main entrance is recessed into an arched vestibule.

The main building is an impressive sight, but it's Cook's glorious tower that makes it memorable. The second floor of the tower features a wheel window with eight cusps. Above it is a segment with ventilators and Italianate brackets, all capped with a church-style steeple. Covering the roof are fish-scale-pattern metal shingles.

Local contractor J. H. Cocke brought Cook's design to life, laying the cornerstone on June 24, 1875. His workers were pulled away for other jobs after fire destroyed most of downtown Senatobia, but he still managed to finish the job in a little more than one year.

The latter years of the nineteenth century and early years of the twentieth were prosperous for Senatobia and Tate County. By 1904, the town had grown to over twelve hundred citizens, and an addition was necessary for the courthouse. Two one-story insets were sympathetically added to close in the original H-shaped plan. In 1975, still more space was added. By the 1990s, despite local care and maintenance, it was obvious that a radical restoration was going to be necessary for the 120-year-old building. Under the direction of architect Belinda Stewart, a faithful renovation was carried out. In December 2000, the newly refurbished Tate County Courthouse was reopened, with the added honor of designation as a Mississippi Landmark.

Designated a Mississippi Landmark, the Tate County Courthouse was extensively renovated in the late 1990s.

CHAMBERLAIN-HUNT ACADEMY

Twenty-three-year-old David Hunt stepped off a riverboat in Natchez in 1801, made his way up the bluffs to his uncle's store, and settled into the life as a businessman in territorial Mississippi. When his uncle died in a duel with George Poindexter, Hunt inherited his store and several estates. With this unexpected windfall, he began to accumulate land and slaves and gradually built his own empire into one of the largest in Mississippi. Eventually, his holdings would earn him the nickname "King David"; he was wealthy beyond imagination even in the rarified atmosphere of the times.

Hunt wasn't a miser; he gave all of his seven children their own plantations and mansions when they married. His generosity extended beyond the family, as well, and he was the prime benefactor of Oakland College during its thirty-year existence. Over a thirteen-year period, Hunt donated more than fourteen thousand dollars to the Presbyterian school, more than twice the amount given by anyone else.

Oakland College was founded and led by Dr. Jeremiah Chamberlain, a Princeton graduate who envisioned this center of learning in one of the most isolated corners of America. Chamberlain laid out a demanding course of study for his pupils and successfully courted deep-pocketed backers such as David Hunt. His murder in the 1850s left the college without its rudder, and it slowly declined before the Civil War.

Following the war, attempts to reopen the college failed. When the legislature offered to buy the campus and establish an agricultural school for freed slaves, the Presbyterian Church readily agreed. The selling price was $21,303.28. Those funds were handed to a Presbyterian board with the stipulation that they be used to found a new school at an undetermined location.

Many towns around Reconstruction Mississippi would have welcomed the economic boost of an educational institution, but Port Gibson claimed the prize. Mindful of the contributions, both financial and academic, made by

David Hunt and Jeremiah Chamberlain, the new school was named Chamberlain-Hunt Academy. It opened in the building that had once housed Brashear Academy, directly behind Port Gibson's famous Presbyterian Church. The 1878 class was delayed by a yellow fever epidemic sweeping through Mississippi, and the school did not officially open until the fall of 1879.

Chamberlain-Hunt was a successful venture from the outset, and it quickly outgrew the Brashear building. The old Woodstock Plantation site was purchased in the 1890s and several outstanding structures were raised to house the academy. McComb Hall was sponsored by a wealthy Chamberlain-Hunt alumnus who had made his fortune in New York. Built in the popular Queen Anne style, it dominated the south side of Port Gibson with its turrets and soaring clock tower. The high-pitched roof was pierced with dormers and tall chimney stacks. Just south of McComb was Guthrie Hall, a three-story dormitory with a broad columned front porch, corner quoins, and a single tall dormer on the front façade.

McComb Hall burned in 1924. Rather than demolish the remaining walls, trustees and alumni of Chamberlain-Hunt elected to rebuild it in a more restrained fashion, consistent with changing architectural trends. The resulting building is a gracious two-story structure with a full raised basement. Flattened arches outline the front porch, and a full-height projecting bay reflects the lost tower.

Chamberlain-Hunt has undergone numerous changes over the past century, including the admission of women beginning in 1970. It still retains a strong military emphasis and greets the children and grandchildren of alumni as new students each year. Guthrie Hall is currently undergoing a multimillion-dollar restoration to house them.

Left: McComb Hall, one of the original buildings on the Chamberlain-Hunt campus, lost its clock tower and turrets in a 1924 fire.

Right: Chamberlain-Hunt was financed by the Presbyterian Church's sale of the Oakland College campus to the State of Mississippi.

FIRST PRESBYTERIAN CHURCH OF OXFORD

IN THE COUNTIES CARVED from the Indian treaty lands of the early 1830s, none was more quickly settled and prosperous than Lafayette. This land that would inspire William Faulkner's tales of Snopeses and Sartorises was lush, inviting, and fertile. When the state legislature awarded Oxford the charter for the proposed university, it just added another feather to the cap of the booming little town.

As with most Mississippi communities in the nineteenth century, Oxford attracted preachers and proselytizers of every stripe. Most drifted through, attracted a handful of converts, and moved on. Generally, a town would wind up with a sprinkling of congregations to meet most needs, including a Baptist church, a Methodist, perhaps an Episcopalian or a Catholic structure. It was rare to find more than one "flavor" of any given denomination, and in

that respect Oxford was unique. Two lively and influential groups of Presbyterians opened their doors in 1837, practically next door to each other on the courthouse square.

The Cumberland Presbyterians were an evangelical offshoot of the mainline Presbyterian Church, drawing most of their membership from Kentucky and Tennessee. They built their first Oxford chapel on the east side of the square, and their pews were soon full. One Oxford matron, dismayed at their growth, observed that "the Cumberlands and the dog fennel are about to take the town."[65]

On the opposite side of the square, the more traditional Presbyterians organized their congregation in July 1837. Unlike the Cumberlands, they struggled with membership and could not even hire a regular preacher until 1838. There was no meeting house until 1843, and then it was just a simple frame chapel with an exterior slave stair leading to the gallery.

Persistence paid off. By 1849, First Presbyterian Church was established enough to attract Dr. John

Oxford's First Presbyterian Church was narrowly saved from Union forces in 1864, only to be demolished by the congregation in the 1880s.

University of Mississippi's first board of trustees was followed by a professorship in 1848.

Dr. Waddel juggled his academic and clerical duties for ten years, much as his contemporary and fellow teacher Frederick A. P. Barnard did at St. Peter's Episcopal Church. Waddel made no secret of his disappointment when the university's vacant chancellorship was awarded to Barnard; his turn at the leadership post would not arrive until after the turmoil of the Civil War.

That war almost destroyed First Presbyterian. Union forces occupied Oxford in 1864, and their arsonous rampage through town left the courthouse, most of the square, and many houses in ruins. Soldiers set fire to First Presbyterian Church, but they were thwarted by Mrs. Henry Rasco, who came racing from her Depot Street home to quench the flames. Ten years later, she led the faction in the church bent on tearing down the 1843 building, causing a bitter rift among the members. Her persistence brought about the demolition of the old church and its replacement with one of the most outstanding examples of Romanesque Revival architecture in Mississippi.

When completed in 1881, the new First Presbyterian Church was a striking red brick structure with a three-story square bell tower, flanked by smaller twin octagonal towers. The side elevations feature engaged stepped buttresses. It towers above the buildings on the west side of the square, having far outlasted its Cumberland rival, which was torn down in the 1940s.

Top: The 1881 First Presbyterian Church of Oxford is a landmark example of Romanesque Revival architecture.

Bottom: First Presbyterian's original sanctuary was a frame chapel with an exterior slave stair, a far cry from the multitowered church now on the site.

Waddel as their full-time pastor. Waddel, one of the first four faculty members at the brand-new University of Mississippi, was an intriguing character. His father had served as president of the University of Georgia, but John had drifted through early careers as a cotton farmer in Alabama and Jasper County, Mississippi. Finding that his father's academic life was more suitable than one behind a plow, he founded Montrose Academy and taught ancient languages there for several years. Appointment to the

DeSoto County Courthouse Murals

Scattered throughout north Mississippi are numerous markers and memorials, each claiming to mark a spot trod by Spanish explorer Hernando de Soto during his march from Alabama to the Mississippi River four hundred years ago. Every one is anecdotal, lacking documentation that anyone of Spanish descent was ever in the neighborhood.

The city of Hernando and DeSoto County may have a more legitimate claim to their namesake's long-lost trail. When the latest DeSoto County Courthouse was being built in the 1940s, excavations turned up an ancient Spanish coin. Another was unearthed in May 1992, and it was dated by the Spanish consul to the late fifteenth century. De Soto and his men may indeed have passed this way, and their exploits are memorably chronicled in a series of murals that now grace the second floor of the courthouse.

The original DeSoto County Courthouse was a simple log hut, built soon after the county was formed from Indian cession lands in the 1830s. A more permanent structure replaced it, but that building was burned by Union troops in 1863. For almost ten years, the county government limped along in the ruined shell of the old courthouse, until Felix LaBauve came home from his native France with plans for a new one. LaBauve, one of Hernando's most prominent citizens, somehow convinced the DeSoto County supervisors to erect a reproduction of a Norman castle on the square.

The towered courthouse, indisputably the most unusual government building in Mississippi, stood until February 1942. Late in the night, fire erupted in the tower, possibly set by an arsonist. Hernandoans raced into the burning structure to save county records, hurling them out the windows. Fire units from Senatobia and Memphis joined the Hernando department, but the courthouse was a total loss. The rubble was hauled away and plans laid for a neoclassical replacement.

The new courthouse was completed within the year. It was just as grand, if not so bizarre, as its predecessor. The interior was notable for a soaring curved rotunda. The architects and designers may not have planned it as a venue

for artwork, but those walls would provide the perfect site for a set of homeless murals that celebrated the history of DeSoto County.

Like much of north Mississippi, Hernando and DeSoto County have always been tied economically and socially to Memphis. Their citizens often traveled to the Tennessee city to shop and dine, and they stayed overnight in famed hotels, from the Peabody to the Chisca to the Gayoso. The latter was one of the oldest and finest; when it burned in 1889, a new Gayoso was built, featuring five huge murals in the lobby. Newton Alonzo Wells painted the scenes of Hernando de Soto discovering the Mississippi River on thirty-inch-wide canvas strips, mounted on panels that are ten feet by twelve feet.

Gayoso patrons admired the murals during the half century that they hung in the lobby. One of the children who marveled at their colorful imagery was J. B. Bell, a Hernando boy who would grow up to be mayor of his hometown. When the Gayoso was renovated by Fred Goldsmith in 1948, the murals were steamed off the walls and discarded. Mayor Bell heard that they had been rejected by the Pink Palace Museum and set out to retrieve them.

By the time DeSoto County's pickup trucks arrived in Memphis, the murals were a damaged, soggy heap. Workers rolled them up like old carpet and threw them in the backs of the trucks, heading south with their treasure.

Top: In 1889 artist Newton Alonzo Wells painted a series of murals for the Gayoso Hotel in Memphis.

Bottom: Wells's panels, ten feet by twelve feet, depict Hernando de Soto's travels through Mississippi in the sixteenth century.

Once they were unfolded, it was apparent that extensive repairs would be necessary. Sam Chezen, a Memphis artist, moved into the DeSoto County Courthouse and set up housekeeping in witness rooms and the attic. He labored over the murals for two years, piecing the paintings back together and restoring the colors.

When Chezen finished his meticulous labor, the murals were carefully mounted on the rotunda walls. They fit as if they had been fashioned for that space. Now, amid the mundane chores of paying taxes and serving jury duty, the people of DeSoto County are treated to a museum-quality art display. Four scenes are depicted: "DeSoto's Embarkation," "Traveling Through the Southern Pines," "Discovery of the Mississippi River," and "Death of DeSoto." A fifth mural, "The Treachery of Tuscaloosa," was considered too graphically violent and was not restored. Smaller mural sections are mounted in the main courtroom and along side hallways.

The murals were again retouched in 1979. Thanks to the talent of Newton Alonzo Wells and Sam Chezen, and the persistence of Mayor J. B. Bell, the DeSoto County Courthouse is a fitting tribute, in name as well as imagery, to the explorer who may have passed by centuries ago.

Top: The DeSoto County Courthouse's rotunda provided the perfect site for the Gayoso's discarded murals.

Bottom: The murals were restored in the late 1940s and retouched in 1979.

VENTRESS BUILDING

OLE MISS'S LYCEUM stands at the top of the Circle, the elliptical green park where the original campus was born. It's austere and formal, an instantly recognizable symbol of the university. This building is all business, befitting the administrative offices within.

At the opposite end of the Circle, as much a part of the lighthearted Grove as the more staid Circle, is the Ventress Building. With its cherry red roof, fairy tale tower, and profusion of gables and angles, it's a marked contrast to every other building on campus.

James Alexander Ventress was the guiding force behind the chartering of the University of Mississippi. He chaired the Educational Finance Committee in the House of Representatives and ramrodded the appropriations bill for a state college through both chambers in 1841. Ventress lived in Woodville, as far as one can travel from Oxford and still remain in Mississippi, but he poured his life's dreams

Ole Miss's Ventress Hall is named for James Alexander Ventress, the Wilkinson County statesman who guided the college's charter through the legislature.

into the school he would rarely see. It would be more than a century before his name would be placed on one of the campus's most elegant buildings.

It was originally the school library, a desperately needed repository for the university's twelve thousand volumes. Over a period of forty years, those books had multiplied from the few on hand when the college opened in 1848. They were crammed and stacked randomly into a single room of the Lyceum. Chancellor Edward V. Mayes wanted that room cleared for other purposes, so he begged and pleaded with the board of trustees until they gave him ten thousand dollars. He hired Memphis architect C. G. Rosenplanter to design an appropriate library building. Oxford contractor W. F. Worley would take those plans and spend the year 1888 bringing them to life.

Rosenplanter had chosen the popular Romanesque Revival style, similar to the design of the new Oxford City Hall rising on the square. The four-story library would have round stone arches, numerous gables and a dominant tubular turret with a tent roof and pointed finial. Windows

Two years after it opened, the library was enhanced with a five-hundred-dollar Tiffany stained-glass window on the north wall of the foyer. The money had been raised by Delta Gamma Sorority girls and college alumni as a tribute to the University Greys.

After just twenty years, the library collection moved on to another building, and the school of law took up residence in the red-roofed structure. Law students would continue the tradition, dating back to the first years of the building's existence, of writing their names on the plaster walls of the stairwell. Many of Mississippi's jurists and judges over the past century could point to the exact spot where they immortalized themselves on the stair, as could Nobel Prize–winning novelist William Faulkner. The tradition continued even after the building was reassigned to the geology department and then the art department.

The Geology Building, as it came to be known, was caught in the midst of campuswide rioting in September 1962. Local clergy climbed the nearby Confederate statue, pleading with students and bystanders for calm and reason as officials brought James Meredith onto campus. Despite tear gas, bullets, and burning cars, the Geology Building was undamaged.

In 1993, the Mississippi legislature appropriated one million dollars to restore and refurbish what would now be called Ventress Hall. It had taken one hundred and fifty years to honor the man responsible for a campus that now educated more than twelve thousand students per year. The renovation was completed in 1998, providing a home for the College of Liberal Arts under the red roof of Ventress.

would follow the curve of the tower's stair to the fourth floor, where three narrow windows pour light into the stairwell. Stone windowsills and lintels add a touch of solidity to the building.

The library was completed in 1889, not a minute too soon for Alice Beynes. The longtime librarian for the university packed all twelve thousand books and hauled them down the Lyceum stairs, across the Circle, and into the new building. With plenty of space, she implemented a much more rational arrangement, easing the task of research for students.

Ventress Hall is famous for its tall, red-roofed turret, where the interior stairwell is covered with generations of students' signatures.

Neshoba County Fairgrounds

For eleven months of the year, the cabins and pavilions of the Neshoba County Fairgrounds sit empty, quietly waiting for the hottest days of summer to roll around. When the gates are unlocked, families whose names can be traced back to the horse-and-buggy era begin to trickle in, stocking their refrigerators with food and sprucing up the dusty porches and sidewalks.

For a week in July, this usually deserted corner of Neshoba County roars to life, drawing in thousands of old-timers, teenagers, politicians, and harness racers. The cabins are filled to overflowing with extended families and their guests, and the entertainment, gossip, and camaraderie roll on from way before sunrise to deep into the night. The Neshoba County Fair fulfills its colloquial role as "Mississippi's Giant Houseparty" year after year.

The roots of today's mega-event stretch back to the late 1800s, when the Grange movement was sweeping through the rural regions of America. This loose organization of farmers and progressives offered the hope of enlightenment and political power for farm families,

and it enjoyed a healthy following in Mississippi. In the summer of 1889, a group of Grangers in Neshoba County decided to hold a low-key fair in the Coldwater community. It was to last just a few hours, with no admission fee, but it drew in several hundred interested patrons. Two of the originators, S. Harrison Parker and W. W. Richardson, laid plans for a bigger and better event the following year.

The 1890 event eclipsed the previous year's fair in attendance and excitement. By 1891, it had expanded to include two full days of horse racing, agricultural exhibits, and entertainment. Not wanting to miss any of the action, families began throwing together small wooden shacks for overnight stays. These tiny cabins enclosed a dusty central square, where the more long-winded speakers naturally gravitated when they felt the need to be heard.

Realizing that they were on to something, nine men incorporated the Stock and Agricultural Fair Association and began selling shares to raise capital. George Harrison donated the twenty acres around the square for a perma-

nent site. The Neshoba County Fair had already become a popular tradition.

A nominal gate fee of twenty-five cents for males over age twelve was initiated in 1892. The charge didn't slow down the crowds, who were already beginning to plan their summer around the event. Harness racing was increasingly popular, and some activities brought disapproving glances from local people. When a frightening storm nearly washed away the 1894 fair, they whispered among themselves that God had brought down retribution on the wicked ways of the fair crowd. The fair association ignored them and proceeded to build a six-hundred-seat pavilion and hotel.

The 1895 fair featured the contest for Best Jackass, as well as cash prizes ranging from fifty cents to two dollars and fifty cents for Best Ox Yoke, Best Ax Handle, and Best Lady Horseback Rider. The following year, Governor Anselm J. McLaurin eagerly accepted an invitation to speak at the Founders Square pavilion, inadvertently starting a tradition that has continued through every administration since.

By 1911, the fair was a firmly entrenched event which pulled in families from all over the state. The original makeshift cabins gave way to more substantial and spacious accommodations, some with two stories and deep

Left: The Neshoba County Fair's midway is an annual tradition that dates back to the earliest years of the fair.

Top right: For one week every summer, harness racing is the sport of choice in Neshoba county.

Bottom right: The first Neshoba County Fair was held in 1889; within just a few years, cabins were being built so families could spend several days at the event.

front porches. Children counted the days until fair time and remembered the anticipation in their later years. Eunice Darby Grubbs recalled the turn-of-the-century summer when she was sixteen years old:

> We left . . . about 4:30 on Tuesday morning . . .
> The children and I got into the wagon . . . We sat in
> the back of the wagon with our feet hanging out the
> back. Just as the sun was peeping up, we went through
> Kenttawka swamp, and as a result of hard driving, we
> reached the fairgrounds before noon. For our food for
> the week, we carried coops of live chickens and trunks
> of fresh vegetables and cakes. If we chose not to use
> our own supplies, we could always rely on the excel-
> lent cooks who worked the fair. There was always the
> opportunity to buy hot biscuits at the restaurant on
> the fairgrounds . . . Of course, there were programs
> each night at the fair under the pavilion. The square
> was then, as it is now, the center of activity. People
> wandered around and around, visiting and talking.
> The late afternoon was really a promenade time dur-
> ing the earlier fairs. People dressed in their very best
> for visiting. I can even remember some people who
> chose evening clothes for their visits.[66]

Mrs. Grubbs's memories would be instantly recogniz-able to patrons of the fair one hundred years later. The same families came each year, adding grandchildren and lament-ing the loss of older generations, renewing friendships that

Hundreds of brightly painted cabins surround Founders Square and line the side streets of the small town that is the Neshoba County Fair.

stretched over decades. The cabins were spruced up each year but not necessarily air-conditioned, even after most of Mississippi came to expect that comfort. Politicians reappeared like fire ants when the pavilion cranked up, and they quickly learned that they skipped the fair at their own peril. Promises were made and tempers flared on Founders Square. Theodore Bilbo bellowed that he would pave every road in Mississippi with bricks, and James K. Vardaman held forth on the evils of racial amalgamation. In the heat and humidity of Neshoba County summer nights, political legends and hopefuls trooped to the pavilion to plead their case and, often, to hurl insults at each other.

There were no insults or amateurs when the fair welcomed presidential hopeful Ronald Reagan on August 3, 1980. Reagan was the front-runner for the Republican nomination and immensely popular in Mississippi. Thirty thousand people crowded into the racetrack grandstands to see the Reagans, who were obviously having the time of their lives. Reagan turned on the charm. "I think all of you know without my saying it that Nancy and I have never seen anything like this, because there isn't anything like this any place else on earth."[67]

Reagan was right. The Neshoba County Fair, from its humble one-day county exhibit origins, had grown into a cultural phenomenon in Mississippi. Each year the crowds grew larger and more cabins were built on the dirt lanes which radiated away from the square. Friendly gamblers hung on the racetrack fences to watch the harness racers fly by, and concerts by entertainers from Patsy Cline to the Spunk Monkeys were preceded by the traditional lawn chair stampede. Generation after generation of politicians wore their wrists out with handshaking and backslapping, making their reputation or slinking off in embarrassed silence after humiliation by a more verbally adept opponent.

The fair has opened its gates every year since that hot summer of 1889, with the exception of the war years from 1942 to 1946. By 1986, all but two of the original cabins were gone, replaced by more comfortable but still rustic houses. But Founders Square remains, and the tradition of hospitality, good food, and good company endures.

TEMPLE GEMILUTH CHASSED

STANDING ON THE WEST SIDE of Port Gibson's appropriately named Church Street is the most unusual ecclesiastical building in Mississippi. Temple Gemiluth Chassed, with its Moorish dome and Byzantine styling, carries the air of an ancient Middle Eastern synagogue, somehow relocated to present-day Claiborne County. The fact that it still exists, long after the last of its congregation moved on, is a miracle in itself.

Religious persecution drove thousands of Jews from Europe's Germanic and Alsace-Lorraine regions in the 1800s. Many headed for America, and a surprisingly large number continued their journey into the American South. Mississippi attracted many of the displaced families, who supported one another and banded together into formal congregations. Woodville, Natchez, Vicksburg, Jackson, Greenwood, Meridian, and other towns counted Jewish

settlers among their most prominent citizens, and many had at least one synagogue or temple.

Most of those temples were similar to the prevailing Christian architecture of the day. A casual observer would have to look carefully to notice the Star of David etched in the glass or the subtle details that indicated the nature of the congregation. But Port Gibson's Jewish conclave elected to build a temple that boldly proclaimed their eastern origins, producing a small gem of a building that was, and is, unique in the state.

The Gemiluth Chassed congregation was formally organized in 1859, though there had been Jewish families in Port Gibson since at least the 1830s. There were twenty-two charter members who met faithfully to observe the Saturday Sabbath in the local Odd Fellows hall and Masonic Lodge. After thirty years of borrowing space, they elected to build a permanent sanctuary, within sight of the famous First Presbyterian Church, the Methodist Church, and the Episcopalians. Congregational presi-

Thirty years after the formation of Congregation Gemiluth Chassed, Port Gibson's Jewish community built an unusual Moorish-style temple.

furnished and entirely finished the cost will be something over $7000. Work will begin at once, and the contract calls for completion of the building by May 1st, 1892. Corner stone will be laid with appropriate ceremonies."[68]

By September 1892, the little temple was finished. It must have generated conversation and curiosity in Port Gibson, for it resembled nothing that native Mississippians had ever seen or imagined. The main doorframe, centered beneath the large onion-shaped dome, was fronted by a curved horseshoe arch. Twin keyhole-shaped arches on either side of the entry simulated windows. Doorways led

Left: An ornate hollow arch provided a setting for the temple's ark and Torah.

Right: With the disappearance of Port Gibson's Jewish families, Temple Gemiluth Chassed fell into extreme disrepair.

dent N. A. Son awarded the contract to J. F. Barnes of Greenville, and work on the temple began in early 1892. The *Port Gibson Reveille* reported the plans but gave no indication of the unique nature of what the temple congregants had in mind: "The contract for the erection of the Jewish synagogue at this place was awarded to J. F. Barnes, of Greenville. The building will be located on the lot between Mr. L. P. Williams' residence and Mr. N. A. Son's store, on Church Street, and will cost $5500. When

off to each side of the vestibule, one opening into a classroom and the other to the rabbi's study. The main room was a spacious auditorium, lit by kerosene chandeliers. Pink and green panes lit the arched windows on each side of the sanctuary. The ark holding the Torah was placed under an ornate hollow metal arch. High above, the red pine ceiling was a masterwork of dark wood, carefully pieced together like a jigsaw puzzle.

Temple Gemiluth Chassed served its thirty families for several decades, even as their numbers began to dwindle. There were still enough members in 1902 for fund-raisers: "The Jewish ladies will give a Japanese luncheon next Wednesday afternoon and night in the parlors of Mr. J. G. Davidson. The luncheon is given for the purpose of having electric lights put in the temple."[69] The Jewish luncheon with a Japanese menu, intended to raise money for lights in a Byzantine Moorish temple, was apparently a success. "The Jewish ladies took in $150 at their Japanese luncheon yesterday. The entertainment was a most enjoyable affair. A beautiful gauze fan, voted to the most popular young lady, was won by Miss Rosa Marx."[70]

The slow but steady Jewish migration out of Mississippi began early in the twentieth century, hitting small towns like Port Gibson especially hard. By midcentury, there was almost no one left to attend services. An unwanted distinction was conferred by the Union of American Hebrew Congregations in the early 1980s: Temple Gemiluth Chassed was their smallest unit, with only four members.

The temple began to deteriorate for lack of use and maintenance, and it was scheduled for demolition in 1986.

Local businessman Bill Lum purchased and stabilized the temple shortly before its planned demolition.

The Torah had been removed to the Goldring/Woldenberg Institute of Southern Jewish Life in Utica, and the century-old synagogue seemed doomed. At the last moment, it was purchased by local businessman Bill Lum. Because of his family's care and attention, and with assistance from the institute, it remains standing and awaiting extensive renovations.

CASTALIAN SPRINGS

IN THE WANING DECADES of the nineteenth century and the early years of the twentieth, well-heeled Mississippi families flocked to spas and resorts scattered around the Magnolia State. Fabled for their "healing" spring waters and serving as a summer haven from the mosquitoes and humidity of plantation life, the resorts featured comfortable hotels, mineral baths, games, and horse racing.

Allison's Wells, Artesian Springs, Cooper's Wells, Lafayette Springs: all are memories now, their buildings long since burned or collapsed. Tastes changed in the 1920s, with more families drawn to the huge new luxury hotels on the Gulf Coast or to more distant destinations, suddenly accessible in new automobiles. The grand old spa hotels were white elephants, unwanted and unused. Most quickly disappeared.

One of the rare remaining spa sites is within a stone's

Castalian Springs is one of the rare remaining spa hotels in Mississippi, which once had dozens of similar sites.

throw of the traffic racing through Holmes County on Interstate 55. Castalian Springs's main structure is a two-story frame hotel with encircling deep porches. Its forty-some-odd rooms all feature screen doors and large windows which allowed breezes into the bedrooms. A long interior hallway leads to a large parlor in the rear, scene of innumerable summer board games and evenings of musical entertainment.

This corner of Mississippi was settled in the 1830s by families from Georgia, the Carolinas, and Alabama. Wesley Chapel, Saron Baptist Church, and Rockey Springs Primitive Baptist were their first churches, and now the graveyards of those churches are all that remain to mark the early settlements.

In 1835, William Allen purchased several acres of land, most likely at the going rate of $1.25 per acre. Five years later, two young boys would stumble across a bubbling spring on the Allen property. The locals deemed the odd-smelling output "healing waters." Some classically

educated soul named the site Castalian Springs, in honor of the ancient pool near the oracle of Delphi. It would be many years before anyone saw the profit potential in the waters.

A boarding school for girls opened near the springs in 1854. Colonel Armistead Otey soon took over the operation; by 1860, he had sixty students in his classrooms. The nearest real town was Durant, which managed to snag a whistle stop on the Mississippi Central Railroad. Castalian Springs itself would never be more than a handful of buildings, but it survived because of its proximity to Durant and the railroad.

Colonel Otey's school, like most other boarding schools in Mississippi, closed its doors with the onset of the Civil War. Anticipating hostilities in the state, the Confederate Army requisitioned the main building for

potential use as a hospital. In April 1862, wounded soldiers from Shiloh and Corinth were brought by rail to Castalian Springs. The long, jarring trip just exacerbated their poor care and horrendous injuries, and many died there. One Kentucky soldier recorded his impressions in his diary:

Corinth, April 20, 1862. Evening sent in ambulance to depot, with other sick, to be sent to Castalian Springs. We had hay put down on the floor of a boxcar to lie down on.

April 21, 1862. Sick, train did not leave Corinth until 6 p.m. Today . . . At Holly Springs, which is a nice place, we stopped for dinner . . . After night got to

The main hotel building at Castalian replaced an identical structure which had burned in 1903.

Durant, our stopping place. By some mistake, our car was taken on to Goodman, or Canton, being asleep, I don't know which, but was brought back by the up passenger. At 11 tonight we are at Durant, still in the car. We passed through many nice little towns today. The country on the railroad is productive, and under high state of cultivation. Saw many pretty ladies.

April 23, 1862. Early went out in town, a small village, and looking cadaverous, a lady called me in and gave me a nice breakfast of milk and bread and etc. While out on this expedition, many ladies had assembled at the cars, with provisions for the sick and wounded. The [Castalian] Springs are three miles from town, and the soldiers were brought out in carriages. About the middle of the forenoon, T. H., Dr. P. and myself, came out in a carriage. The boys had a bottle of 'hoosletter' and were quite merry. I am in a room on the 2nd floor, occupied by 'Morgan's men,' the boys I came with, belonging to that 'layout.' Morgan's men are quite a curiosity to the people down here . . . The building is a two-story frame with 'wings,' 'ells,' etc., and is accommodating nearly three hundred sick and wounded—nearly all Kentuckians. The grounds are tastefully arranged about the springs, and the scenery, in the vicinity, is romantic. There was lately a female school kept in this place—was broken up, to convert the building into a hospital. The principal is our stewart [sic]. The water of the springs is chalybeate. This evening had some pleasant conversation with ladies.

April 24, 1862. When I got up this morning, I walked out on the upper gallery, and could look down on the preparations for breakfast, the tables being set out in the yard . . . I did not like the appearance of the bacon and corn bread . . . I proposed to T. H. and D. P. to walk out a short distance in the country and get breakfast . . . In about a half a mile we came to quite a humble looking residence, but on stopping at the gate, we were invited in and treated with great hospitality. The lady's husband was in the army, and she thought it very strange we did not know him. The old pipe-smoking grandmother was in the corner, and she held up her hands in wonder, when informed that we had never met her sons, John and 'Jeems,' who were in the Virginia army.

May 5, 1862. [A]m not well, time drags heavily—nothing to read. Next day improving.

May 14, 1862. Brown died in our room this morning. How little feeling soldiers have sometimes. Though ever willing to help a comrade while living, when dead, there is never much shedding of tears for them. We were all standing around Brown's bed, and when he drew his last breath, one of the boys bent over him, and said, 'He never will draw another breath as long as he lives.' This was said so simply, the whole room roared out in laughter. We buried B. in the evening. Many are dying here. Intend to go to the front in a few days. Tomorrow we start for Corinth.[71]

Martha Ann Otey, wife of the school's owner, cleared out a spot near Wesley Chapel where the soldiers could be buried. The first grave was dug for Sammy Orzon of Arkansas, who died on May 16, 1862. Over the next few weeks, the little cemetery grew more crowded, with forty-two fellow Confederates joining Orzon. Mrs. Otey had the sad duty of overseeing the cemetery for the next few months. When her attempts to reopen the school failed, she moved to Texas. Colonel Otey's fate is not known.

Mississippi finally developed a public education system in the 1870s, and very few of the antebellum boarding schools reopened. This left Castalian Springs with a very large, very empty building and no business. Some enterprising soul recognized the trend toward resort vacations and transformed the old school into a hotel. With its lush setting, bubbling waters, and proximity to the increasingly prosperous Delta region, Castalian Springs Resort was a success. As outbuildings were added, it could accommodate several hundred guests at a time. Coaches would meet the trains in Durant and ferry arrivals to the inn, where they were treated to mineral baths, tournaments of all sorts, horseback riding, gambling, and cock fighting.

Castalian Springs thrived through the heyday of Mississippi's turn-of-the-century spa period. In 1903, the main building burned, but it was quickly replaced with an identical structure. It prospered for a few more years, but eventually met the same fate as Stafford Springs, Owen's Wells, and others. The arrival of paved highways and affordable cars gave families more options for their spare time, and the grand new beach hotels in Gulfport, Biloxi, and Pass Christian were just too much of a draw for the spas to be able to compete effectively.

The hotel was empty for years before being purchased by the Jackson YMCA in the 1950s. It was an ideal location and layout for a girls' summer camp, and for more than twenty years, it welcomed hundreds of campers for archery, crafts, fishing, and swimming. Cabins were scattered through the wooded hillsides, and campfires inspired ghostly tales of the Confederate general who roamed the upstairs hallway of the old hotel building.

With the demise of Camp Castalian, the hotel was once again empty and endangered. New Tribes Missions, an evangelistic training program for foreign missionaries, took it over in the 1970s and maintained the main building and cabins for almost thirty years. Local genealogical researchers rediscovered Mrs. Otey's little cemetery and cleaned up the Civil War graves.

The missionaries have moved on. Healing waters have lost their charm, and summer camps have found new locations. When the autumn winds strip the trees just east of Castalian Springs, the century-old hotel can still be spotted, waiting for new owners and a new purpose.

CENTRAL FIRE STATION

For the first ten years of its existence, Jackson had no real need for anything resembling a fire department. Very few houses were built, none of any size or noteworthy architectural style, and the only government building standing was a small statehouse on the corner of President and Capitol streets. By 1830, many of the legislators who dreaded the yearly trek to the muddy, miasmic capital city may have wished that it would burn down and be replaced by Vicksburg, Columbus, or Natchez.

The 1832 Constitution allowed Jackson eighteen years to clean up its act. Long before that deadline, city boosters pushed through funding for a state capitol, the Governor's Mansion, the State Penitentiary, and other public buildings. With civic stability, fine homes began to appear along State Street, and businessmen invested in brick stores, hotels, and taverns.

Increased prosperity brought increased financial risks, including that of fire, the bane of many a nineteenth-century town. Jackson Fire Company No. 1 was formed in 1830, followed by several other groups of quasi-professional

firefighters. These early firemen, all amateurs, managed to keep most of Jackson standing until the Civil War, when their ranks were decimated by military obligations and the wholesale abandonment of the city in the face of Union advancement.

Occupied by Federal troops several times in 1863, Jackson emerged with the unflattering nickname "Chimneyville." Some buildings, primarily those with war-related functions, were intentionally torched. Others were simply victims of overzealous soldiers or unfortunate proximity to exploding factories and munition sites. Regardless of the origins, flames swept through much of Jackson, and photos from the postwar period show burned-out shells of hotels, churches, and homes.

Within thirty years, a new, more elegant Jackson had arisen on the ashes of the old. Fire equipment was becoming more sophisticated, and voters insisted on the best available protection for their property. With those demands in mind, the mayor and aldermen voted on June 7, 1904, to establish a full-time professional fire department. At their

meeting on September 6, 1904, they laid plans for a suitable fire station:

> Your building committee, after investigating the conditions of the fire buildings and the cost of repairing them, and taking into consideration the services required of a fireman . . . think it would improve the service and be cheaper, to concentrate the fire equipment from the three buildings, formally known as the Gem No. 2, Jackson No. 1, and the Hope No. 3, in one building. We therefore recommend that a three-story brick building, 60 x 80 feet in size, be erected in the City Hall lot; said building in addition to providing for places for the men and apparatus and horses should have a place in the battery room for the alarm system and the large bell now at the Century [*sic*] School Building should be placed on it.[72]

Controversy raged for several months over the site for the new Central Fire Station. One group felt that the north side of the Jackson City Hall lot was the logical site; another pushed for the Old Capitol Green. In 1904, city hall was still a functioning government building, but the Old Capitol had been abandoned for the new statehouse and was slowly moldering away on the Green. After much discussion, it was decided to build the station next to city hall, perhaps with the notion that a fire in that building would be much more damaging than in the drafty Old Capitol.

The postwar boom in Jackson necessitated a centrally located firehouse, which was finished in 1904.

Patrick Henry Weathers was hired to serve as architect for the fire station. He was an Alabama native who practiced his craft for an unknown number of years in Mississippi, leaving the state with such landmarks as the Carroll County Courthouse in Vaiden, the Lee County Courthouse in Tupelo, and St. Peter's Catholic and St. Andrew's Episcopal churches in Jackson. For Central Fire Station, he fashioned a three-story stucco-over-brick block with classic elements. Pilasters divide the front façade bays, their capitals providing an entablature which separates the ground floor from the upper stories. An unbroken parapet rises from a metal cornice, and a belfry tower originally rose above the northeast corner. It was that tower which housed the old Central High School bell, its clapper ringing out whenever the fire wagons and horses came thundering out of the big double doors.

Central Fire Station was completed in 1904 and soon housed a state-of-the-art horse-drawn steam-powered pumper, "No. 691." It was likely still in use when the firemen began taking in stray animals and donated pets from around Jackson. By 1919, their odd menagerie included rabbits, squirrels, monkeys, guinea pigs, alligators, and deer. With limited space in the fire station, the city moved the collection to newly opened Livingston Park, situated on seventy-nine acres on West Capitol Street. From the firemen's benevolence grew the Jackson Zoo.

As Jackson expanded throughout the twentieth century, more and more outlying fire stations were built, and the downtown station became increasingly dated and outmoded. It was finally closed in the 1970s and later refurbished to house the city's visitors' bureau.

Mississippi Industrial College

Of all the counties carved from the 1830 Indian cession lands, none was more prosperous than Marshall. Before the town of Holly Springs was even incorporated, new settlers had pooled their resources to plan a school. Chalmers Institute, Holly Springs Female Institute, St. Thomas Hall, and Maury Institute were recognized as some of the state's finest academies in the antebellum era.

Just north of Holly Springs, the Cottrell brothers of Sylvestria Plantation sponsored male and female academies. They may have even defied Mississippi law and public sentiment and allowed their slaves to obtain some rudimentary education. Elias Cottrell, who grew up in slavery at Sylvestria, would eventually lead hundreds of his fellow freedmen out of illiteracy and ignorance.

Following the Civil War, northern missionary groups poured manpower and resources into Mississippi in an

The Carnegie Foundation provided the funds for what was, for many years, Mississippi's largest meeting space under African American control.

effort to raise the level of literacy and skills for newly freed blacks. Natchez College was such a rousing success that it outgrew its campus and relocated to Jackson. It shared space with Millsaps College before moving on to Lynch Street and development into Jackson State University. Tougaloo College began in the old plantation manor of John Boddie, just north of Jackson. Shaw University was opened by the Methodist Church and would be renamed Rust College in 1892.

These schools thrived through the 1880s, providing hope for a generation that had previously known none. The rise of Jim Crow laws and the race-baiting rhetoric of politicians like James K. Vardaman and Theodore Bilbo slowed their growth and threatened their very existence. By 1900, most blacks had lost their right to vote and become entangled in the cruel sharecropping system. College was once again only a dim dream for most.

The politics and prejudices of the day add to the remarkable success story that was initiated by Elias

Cottrell in 1905. This former Sylvestria Plantation slave boy had taught himself Hebrew and Greek, attained a degree in theology, and risen to the bishopry of the Colored Methodist Episcopal Church. Realizing the practical needs of his people, as well as their hunger for formal education, Bishop Cottrell fashioned an institute where black students could pursue theology, vocational training, and music lessons. Teaming with leaders of both races in Holly Springs, he raised fifty-three hundred dollars and purchased a 110-acre tract of land on the northern edge of town. Included in that tract was the antebellum home of the Mills family, wealthy planters and merchants.

The old Mills house would be the core of the primary building for Mississippi Industrial College. Board minutes from 1905 record that members voted ten thousand dollars to repair the structure, but it is unclear how much of the original house, beyond the easily recognized Greek Revival frontispiece, was preserved. The resulting structure, Catherine Hall, served as the women's dormitory and included formal parlors, the matron's office, and classrooms for music, domestic arts, and domestic science. The

Catherine Hall, Hammond Hall, and the Carnegie Auditorium of Mississippi Industrial College are boarded up and decaying.

exterior is an exuberant Jacobean style, with two projecting gable-roof pavilions, curvilinear parapet walls, and finials. The pavilions were once connected by a frame portico, complete with Roman Doric columns and an entablature, but that section has long since rotted away.

MIC opened in January 1906, and by the end of the first session boasted an enrollment of two hundred students. Bishop Cottrell's vision pulled in more and more eager young people, and additional buildings began to fill the Mills plantation site. Hammond Hall, designed to mirror Catherine Hall's Jacobean style, housed male students. Washington Hall was finished in 1910, at a cost of forty thousand dollars.

The crowning architectural element of MIC's campus was the Carnegie Auditorium, financed in large part by a twenty-five-thousand-dollar grant from the Andrew Carnegie Foundation. The foundation was noted for building libraries all over America, and this was the only public meeting space which they funded in Mississippi. Towering over the campus, it is a two-and-a-half-story brick building with a raised basement plan. Classroom wings stretch north and south of the main wing, whose height is emphasized by a two-story entrance portico and pedimented roof. The auditorium seats two thousand, making it by far the largest meeting space in an African American institution in the pre–civil rights era. A 1930 fire caused severe damage to the building, but it was restored and used until the school closed.

Mississippi Industrial College served a vital role in educating black students for most of the twentieth century. It survived in the shadow of the larger and more diverse Rust College, and its mission gradually evolved into one of teachers' training and business management. During World War II, when a teacher shortage threatened the already-struggling black public school system, MIC joined the Rural School Project, where its students could earn college credits by living and teaching in rural communities.

The civil rights era opened up vast opportunities for minority students, including admission to all of Mississippi's universities and community colleges. MIC was one of the unintended victims of that social upheaval, and its student body slowly dwindled. The doors were locked for good in the early 1980s. Elias Cottrell's campus now stands quiet and forlorn, its buildings crumbling bit by bit. Catherine Hall is a dangerously derelict shell. Hammond Hall and Washington Hall are boarded up, as is the proud Carnegie Auditorium. One of the more modern buildings houses a few offices and shops, but the future of the original structures is uncertain.

LEFLORE COUNTY COURTHOUSE AND CONFEDERATE MONUMENT

THE YAZOO RIVER is born at the far northeast boundary of the city of Greenwood, where the Tallahatchie and Yalobusha converge. It swings in a wide arc, reversing the easterly flow of the Tallahatchie to a western route, and snakes right through the middle of Greenwood. The point where it slips beneath Keesler Bridge is one of Indian legends. The Choctaws revered this as a sacred site and administered their justice on the banks, tossing the condemned into the muddy, rolling tide of the river. "Yazoo" translates to "River of Death" in their language.

The Choctaws are long gone, but their site remains the seat of local justice. A small courthouse was built here soon after Leflore County was created from parts of Sunflower, Carroll, and Tallahatchie counties. That 1871 structure was brick, topped by a cupola, and adequate for the population of a small river community.

The Leflore County Courthouse's Confederate Monument is the most ornate in Mississippi, with six individual marble statues.

Thirty years later, it was evident that a grander courthouse was going to be needed. Greenwood was in the catbird seat of the Delta's turn-of-the-century cotton boom, and its streets were lined with the offices of cotton brokers, attorneys, and businessmen. The castle-like Davis Primary School was under construction, and boats were lined up along the Yazoo's banks to carry off cotton bales by the thousands. The population would more than double in the first decade of the new century, from three thousand to seven thousand.

The 1871 courthouse was demolished, and in its place rose one of the most enduring examples of Beaux Arts architecture in Mississippi. Famed Chattanooga architect R. H. Hunt fashioned a massive two-story rectangular block with a balustraded mansard roof. The façades were surfaced in smooth-faced ashlar blocks, and a full-height pedimented entrance with Ionic columns added to the effect. Topping it all was a three-stage tower with four clock faces, visible from all corners of Greenwood.

The new courthouse was completed in 1906. Twenty years later, the original block was extended back almost to the riverbank, adding office and jail space. East and west wings were added to the front in 1953. The additions were sympathetic to the original and combined to produce an enormous, imposing structure that dominated downtown Greenwood.

The first years of the courthouse coincided with a remarkable "Lost Cause" movement sweeping through Mississippi and other former Confederate states. Local groups, such as the United Daughters of the Confederacy and Sons of Confederate Veterans, had been placing monuments in every little town and crossroads during the 1890s and early 1900s. Most were stock pieces, usually a lone sentry with a rifle, perched atop a simple obelisk. The statues were traditionally placed on the courthouse lawn, although a few were inexplicably deposited in the middle of a downtown intersection.

Greenwood had an unusually active and determined UDC chapter. Through their efforts, the only Confederate Memorial Building in Mississippi was funded, but this didn't satisfy their need to commemorate. These indomitable ladies contracted with Columbus Marble Works to fashion the largest and most heavily populated Confederate monument in the state, perhaps in the South. The Leflore County Board of Supervisors, possibly in an effort to maintain peace in their own homes, appropriated five thousand dollars to "aid in the making, building and erection of said monument, and [they] set apart the southeast corner of said courthouse square for the purpose of having said monument erected thereon."[73] The base, sunk two feet into the soil, was "to be built and made of the best personally selected flawless silver gray Georgia marble." The figures themselves "shall be cut out of the best perfect Italian marble, cut in Italy."

It would take more than a year for the base to be finished and the statues carved. When all was said and done, six marble figures crowded the monument at multiple levels. They were kept under wraps until October 9, 1913, when six hundred Confederate veterans gathered on the Leflore County Courthouse lawn. Girls in white dresses

The three-stage Leflore County Courthouse clock tower was designed by Chattanooga architect R. H. Hunt.

and elaborate sashes performed a complicated drill to whisk away the drapes, revealing the monument. Photos of the day show a sea of people on the lawn, crowding the street and even perched on nearby rooftops.

The tableau that debuted that day, which still stands on the corner of the courthouse square, was a busy one. At the top of the monument stands a Confederate officer, placed there in honor of General B. G. Humphreys, who would serve a tumultuous term as Mississippi's first Reconstruction governor. Beneath him are five figures, distributed among the four compass points. Facing south is an artilleryman, surrounded by stacked cannonballs, grasping his cannon rammer. On the opposite side, a soldier strides forward, drawing his sword as he goes. On the courthouse side is a woman with hands kneaded together, described in the contract as "a sure enough woman," with no hint of angelic origins. She is modeled after Sallie Morgan Kimbrough Clements. Facing east is a rare double figure, with a kneeling woman tending to a young soldier. This little drama was dedicated to the memory of Lewis Sharkey Morgan, killed at age fifteen in the Battle of Collierville. His niece, Mrs. L. P. Yerger, and his great-nephew, William Morgan Kimbrough, posed for the figures.

In 1933, Lizzie George Henderson donated a set of Westminster chimes to the county in memory of her husband. The chimes were engineered to ring each quarter hour, sequentially adding the lines of the Westminster Prayer until the verse was complete on the hour. Their familiar tones became a symbol of Greenwood and were subconsciously incorporated into the memories of generations of Deltonians.

Over the past century, the Leflore County Courthouse and its monument have endured challenges and the ravages of age. The clock mechanism gradually rusted and, for years, all four faces showed random time settings. Even the Westminster chimes ground to a halt and were silent. The worst blow was struck when civil engineers discovered large cavities beneath the Yazoo riverbank, eroding the soil beneath the courthouse and threatening to topple the whole pile into the water. With some degree of urgency, the entire county government was moved to the old hospital, and machinery and mechanical minds united to shore up the failing levee.

At its century mark, the Leflore County Courthouse has been stabilized and is a vibrant, well-preserved landmark. The clockworks have been repaired and the chimes once again toll every fifteen minutes. The Confederate Monument still supports its little army of stone soldiers and stalwart women, a bit worse for wear but enduring, symbols of a Lost Cause and a lost time.

ILLINOIS MONUMENT

IN THE SPACE OF A FEW miserable weeks of 1863, Vicksburg was transformed from a vibrant, thriving river city into a nightmarish world of siege, cave life, and trench warfare. For almost two months, General John C. Pemberton's Confederates dug in and hung on, battling overwhelming odds and superior numbers as Union troops pounded them across siege lines and from gunboats moored in the Mississippi River. Casualties were astounding, and bodies were hastily piled into trenches for burial. Shells cratered the hillsides, and mounds of earth thrown up for fortifications altered the topography of this once gracious town.

The siege finally ended on July 4, 1863, coinciding with General Robert E. Lee's retreat from Gettysburg. The Confederacy never recovered from these twin blows, and many historians attribute the more serious damage to the Vicksburg campaign. The war would drag on for two more painful years, a time when the soldiers' bodies

Thousands of Illinois veterans and supporters traveled to Vicksburg for the 1906 dedication of their monument.

scattered around Vicksburg were reburied and the townspeople cautiously crept out of their caves and back to their shell-pocked homes.

Largely because of its strategic location on the Mississippi, Vicksburg bounced back economically much faster than the rest of the state in the postwar period. Forward-thinking Vicksburgers had turned their collective back on the thousands of acres where the fighting took place, ignoring the gulleys still full of spent minie balls and rusting bayonets. They were looking to a brighter future and saw no need to venerate the site of so much suffering and violence.

Thirty years passed. The New South emerged from war and Reconstruction, and Vicksburg prospered, as did much of America. With the passage of time, the old battlefields in Virginia, Georgia, and Tennessee were seen as sacred ground, and the thousands of veterans of the Vicksburg siege, northerners and southerners alike, slowly realized that, without their input, future generations would have no knowledge of what had transpired there.

Colonel C. C. Floweree, who had made his fortune by cornering the lucrative ice market in western Mississippi, was a veteran, ironically, of the Gettysburg campaign. Although he had missed the battle action in Vicksburg, he utilized his financial resources and persuasive talents to organize a huge reunion of veterans in his hometown, calling back aging warriors from all corners of America. They eagerly descended on the hills and fields of their youth, pointing out entrenchments and the locations of significant turning points in the battle.

That 1890 reunion sparked a groundswell of sentiment for a national park. The old soldiers wanted to be remembered for their valor, and military historians were confirming Vicksburg's pivotal role in Civil War lore. With backing from their congressmen, the veterans lobbied for the establishment of the Vicksburg National Military Park.

President William McKinley signed the enabling act in 1895, and local landowners donated almost two thousand acres of private property back to the government. Guided by the men who had been there during the worst of the fighting, workers began landscaping the hills and clearing out the valleys for the park.

The national park movement generated excitement all over the country. As a new century dawned, waves of nostalgia for the Lost Cause and the Grand Army of the Republic were sweeping the nation, with almost every little crossroads and village dedicating a courthouse monument or memorial plaque. The Sons of Confederate Veterans, United Daughters of the Confederacy, and complementary northern groups sponsored parades, hung banners, and raised funds for state monuments at Gettysburg, Shiloh, and Antietam. The Civil War was suddenly fashionable again, and Vicksburg was climbing on the bandwagon.

Not everyone in Mississippi was enthusiastic about the military park. State legislators looked at the project with a jaundiced eye, resentful of land being returned to the federal government to commemorate a still-painful loss. Governor Andrew Longino sniffed at the planned memorials and labeled them "rot." General Stephen D. Lee, a decorated veteran of the Vicksburg campaign and the first Vicksburg National Military Park commissioner, pled with lawmakers to sponsor a Mississippi memorial, but it would be ten years after the park's official dedication before the Magnolia State would be represented there.

Many northern legislatures were understandably

The seal of the State of Illinois is inlaid in a marble mosaic beneath the dome of the monument.

more open to the idea of sponsoring memorials at the site of their side's grand victory. Iowa, New Hampshire, Massachusetts, Wisconsin, and Ohio all jumped in with elaborate plans for statues, plaques, and signage. They were all overshadowed by Illinois, the state which had sent more troops than any other to Vicksburg. Throughout the "land of Lincoln," Grand Army of the Republic veterans' groups petitioned legislators and held fund-raisers for what they hoped would be a worthy memorial to their fallen comrades.

In 1901, the Illinois legislature appointed a commission to oversee site selection and design of a Vicksburg monument. Because they were one of the first states to sign on, they had their choice of prime locations. They selected a commanding hill just beyond the ruined Shirley House, the only extant antebellum structure within the park's boundaries. With a $260,000 appropriation in hand, the Illinois team laid out plans for a replica of Rome's Pantheon, a masterpiece of marble and granite which would dominate the vista.

Illinois's veterans were determined to have the premier monument in the park, and by anyone's standards, they got their wish. The Illinois Monument is a round structure of gleaming Georgia marble, approached by forty-seven wide Stone Mountain granite steps. Six twenty-foot columns support the portico, on which are carved three female figures. These represent "History" recording the deeds of "The North" and "The South." Topping the portico is a bronze eagle, gilded with gold leaf. A frieze band loops

The Illinois Monument is a tribute to the thirty-six thousand troops of that state who fought at Vicksburg.

around the monument, bearing a quote from Illinois's favorite son, Abraham Lincoln.

The entrance to the interior is guarded by two huge bronze doors. Marble mosaic floors bear the seal of the State of Illinois, and sixty bronze tablets encircle the floor, carved with the names of thirty-six thousand state soldiers who served at Vicksburg. The curved ceiling soars fifty-five feet, with an opening at the apex. Local legend holds that it never rains through the aperture.

Dedication of the gleaming new building was slated for October 26, 1906, eleven years after the Vicksburg National Park Association was formed. Chartered trains rolled in from Illinois, carrying veterans, politicians, and two thousand proud citizens of the state, many on their first visit to the South. They paraded from the downtown Vicksburg depot to the park, where Mississippi governor

James K. Vardaman welcomed them. Mindful of the conflict raging in his own legislature, Vardaman promised the northern visitors that Mississippi would one day boast a monument as well, "not as costly, or as fine as yours, but it will be as fine as the state of Mississippi can afford."[74]

Mississippi's monument was finally approved and installed in 1912. It is an impressive granite obelisk, dominated by a statue of Clio, the muse of history, recording the names of Mississippi's sons in her book. But grand as it is, and memorable as many of the other state memorials around the park are, none compares to the Illinois Monument, its granite and marble still gleaming in the Warren County sun after a century. It's the first major monument today's traveler encounters in the park, and it sets the tone of reverence that the people of Illinois strived to achieve.

Our Lady of the Gulf Catholic Church

On the far western edge of the Mississippi Gulf Coast, the Mississippi Sound makes a sweeping curve and merges into the Bay of St. Louis. The land along this shoreline attracted Indians hundreds of years before the first French explorers paddled up, and they established a village known as Achoupoulou. Pierre Le Moyne, Sieur d'Iberville understood their affection for the area, one of the most enticing in the entire gulf region.

The city of Bay St. Louis developed as a convenient weekend and summer resort for New Orleanians. They built their cottages and beach houses to catch the cooling breezes of the gulf, and their laid-back ambience became a hallmark of Bay St. Louis over several centuries.

The influence of the French and Louisiana residents left Bay St. Louis with a large Catholic population, rare in antebellum Mississippi. When Pope Gregory XVI blessed the Diocese of Natchez in 1837, the need for a pastor in coastal Mississippi was evident. Bishop Chanche appointed Father Louis Stanislaus Mary Buteaux to the post, a fortuitous move for the coast's religious and educational future.

Father Buteaux spent twelve years in Bay St. Louis, leaving a legacy that is still evident today. He built the first chapel for Our Lady of the Gulf Catholic Church in 1848, and opened St. Stanislaus College for boys in 1854 and St. Joseph's Academy for girls in 1855. Both Our Lady of the Gulf and St. Stanislaus remain, but St. Joseph's closed in 1967.

Father Buteaux was succeeded by another dedicated and long-serving priest, Father Henry LeDuc. Born in France, Father LeDuc was ordained there and then immediately set sail for Bay St. Louis. It would be his only parish, where he would labor for almost forty years. When Union soldiers threatened to burn Bay St. Louis, he met them with the Cross of Christ held over his head. Realizing that they were in more danger from this indomitable priest than from the few Confederate troops in town, they retreated.

A number of priests served Our Lady of the Gulf after the death of Father LeDuc in 1897. On November 16, 1907, Father John Prendergast watched with most of Bay St. Louis's population as fire consumed the church, its rectory, and St. Joseph's Academy. By the next fall, a new cornerstone was being laid, and the present chapel was opened within months.

The 1908 church is a stunning example of ecclesiastic architecture, with a three-story square clock tower, arched windows, and a full formal portico. Inside, stained-glass windows feature musical instruments, and the ceiling is a vivid blue bordered in brown. The altar is carved from Italian Carrerra marble. High above it is a painting of Mary, depicted as Our Lady of the Gulf.

The church's location on the beach road, surrounded by live oaks, lends an air of serenity and beauty to the site. That serenity was broken on August 29, 2005, when Bay St. Louis took a direct hit from Hurricane Katrina. Our Lady of the Gulf suffered massive damage, as did almost every structure in the community. But unlike many of its neighbors, the chapel survived and is currently undergoing extensive renovations.

Left: Our Lady of the Gulf, severely damaged by Hurricane Katrina, stands in Bay St. Louis as a symbol of rebirth and renewal.

Right: The 1908 Our Lady of the Gulf Catholic Church replaced an 1848 structure lost to fire.

GREENWOOD'S GRAND BOULEVARD

WITH THE DEVELOPMENT of an effective levee system, the arrival of the railroads, improved farming techniques, and more durable cotton strains, Mississippi welcomed a second "cotton kingdom" in the late 1800s and early 1900s. The first cotton boom had centered around old towns like Natchez, Vicksburg, and Holly Springs, but this resurgence would be concentrated in the Mississippi Delta.

No town prospered more from the rebirth of the cotton economy than Greenwood. Even a century later, the effects of those riches can be seen in the architectural grandeur of the Leflore County Courthouse, the Keesler Bridge, downtown storefronts, and the newly refurbished Alluvian Hotel.

River Road was the preferred address for the domestic showplaces built with cotton money. As its lots filled with neoclassical houses, developers began to look north of the

Yazoo for open land. The tiny village of North Greenwood, incorporated in 1906 with a population of 127, was a logical site. An iron bridge connected downtown Greenwood with its much smaller neighbor, surrounded on all sides by cotton fields of the J. Z. George plantation. That plantation was hundreds of acres of flat, open vistas stretching all the way from the Yazoo to the Tallahatchie River.

Captain Sam Gwin, E. R. McShane and W. L. Loggins bought up most of the plantation and began platting estate-size lots, all fronting on a broad street they dubbed Grand Boulevard. Each parcel would encompass up to ten acres, with smaller lots available on side streets. The first deals were closed in 1910, as buyers eagerly anticipated life in the Boulevard Subdivision.

It would have been just another street in a small Mississippi town, albeit one with a grandiose name, if not for Captain Gwin's wife. Sally Humphreys Gwin was the granddaughter of Reconstruction governor Benjamin Humphreys, and she apparently inherited that forebear's iron will and determination. Where her husband and his partners saw profit, she saw a flat, boring road lined with houses that deserved a more intriguing landscape. In her mind, it was truly a grand boulevard, destined to be lined with towering oaks. But there were no trees to work with in the midst of acres and acres of cotton fields. That was just a bothersome detail to Mrs. Gwin. She rounded up her husband's foreman, Horace Greeley Austin, and laid out a plan that would transform North Greenwood forever.

Greeley Austin was a young man who was used to hard work, but he had never encountered the likes of Sally Gwin. With her husband, she rode the riverbanks along the Tallahatchie and marked chosen oak saplings with north-facing blazes. Greeley would then uproot the trees, place them in deep water buckets, and haul them down the boulevard. Carefully spaced and supported by crossbeams, they were lowered into the freshly dug holes, their blazes still pointing north.

The work went on for more than six years. Greeley recalled his labors a half century later:

> We got the trees—from the very start—at different places: Walker Lake . . . [the] Loggins place along the river bank . . . a little patch of woods there now by Pillow school . . . some from Mr. Paul Montjoy's place, east of town . . . Both Mr. Sam and Miss Sally oversee'd the trees, but Miss Sally was out there most. I was responsible to see that the trees were the right distance apart and was in a straight line. Mr. Sam would stand there looking down the line and he would call me and say "Greeley, that tree is out of line," or it was too close to the other tree. He would

come along some day and say "Set that tree out, but some day we're going to have to cut it down." I didn't know what he was talking about, but he was talking about putting in the side streets . . . We hauled the water in three or four barrels in a wagon. The men worked all night watering the trees. Mr. Sam's orders were to water the trees at night—not every night. It would take a week to get around.[75]

Greeley broke down one night in tears, exhausted and at wit's end when none of the day's blazes could be found on the young trees.

Most of the oak trees were transplanted from 1916 to 1922, but the last ones were not in place until the 1950s. The Gwins built their own house in 1917 on the highest lot on the boulevard, halfway between the two rivers. While it was under construction, Mrs. Gwin led a daily entourage on foot across the old iron Yazoo River bridge to inspect the trees and the house. With her big floppy hat and her five small children, she was a familiar sight to the citizens of North Greenwood. Most of the trees were thriving, and in her mind they were already arching across the brick boulevard and meeting high above the street in a mile-long unbroken parade.

"Miss Sally's oaks" would grow to be Greenwood's most famous landmark. They survived the flood of 1932, when the Tallahatchie River jumped its banks and came roaring straight down the boulevard. The water remained waist-deep for weeks, but the social-conscious Grand Boulevard inhabitants refused to let it interfere with the spring party season. Old photos from that year show fashionably dressed young women being poled through the floodwaters in boats, their best shoes and dress hems tucked carefully into buckets.

Over several decades, the lots along Grand Boulevard came to feature some of the finest architecture in the Delta. The Neoclassic Provine House, Spanish Eclectic Bledsoe House, and Tudor-style Hobbes House joined smaller bungalows and classically southern homes to make this a visual delight. The oldest house on the boulevard, a Victorian farmhouse which originally stood in the middle of the proposed road, was jacked up on logs and hauled to its new location by mules. Ironically, the workers set it down facing a side street rather than the boulevard, and it remains there today, the only house on the road to face south rather than east or west.

Sally Gwin lived the rest of her life in the family manor at the corner of Grand Boulevard and Park Avenue. She faithfully tended her trees for decades and was lauded by the Department of the Interior for her part in what the *New York Times* once described as the "Most Beautiful Street in America." She died in the midst of a violent 1950s storm, listening to the sound of the giant limbs crashing onto the boulevard.

The Boulevard Subdivision is now approaching the end of its first century, and many of the original trees have succumbed to wind and age. But there are still quite a few standing, identifiable by their massive circumference and their roots, which twist and buck underneath the sidewalks. Recent repaving revealed the original brick roadway and the outline of the wide median that Captain Gwin laid down. Miss Sally's house, much altered, still occupies the high point of the boulevard as a testament to an indomitable and farsighted woman.

WALTER PLACE GARDENS

IN HOLLY SPRINGS, a town that seems to have an outstanding antebellum mansion on every corner, Walter Place is a head turner. Dominating West Chulahoma Street, its massive Greek Revival columns and twin Gothic towers are unlike anything else in Mississippi. Colonel Harvey Washington Walter intended for his home to be noticed, and for more than one hundred and fifty years, it has been.

Colonel Walter's home was designed by Spires Boling for maximum impact. It was larger and more unusual than most other houses and was filled with an exuberant and talented family. Walter was the driving force behind the Mississippi Central Railroad, Whig candidate for governor in 1859, an outspoken opponent of secession, and a gracious host to Mrs. Ulysses Grant during the occupation of Holly Springs. In 1878, he evacuated his wife, infant son, and daughters to Alabama as yellow fever decimated the

Oscar Johnson's German landscaper laid out acres of gardens around Walter Place in the early 1900s.

town, remaining behind with his other three sons during the crisis. All four of the Walter men died.

Walter Place passed to his widow and was purchased by her son-in-law, Oscar Johnson, in 1889. Johnson and his brother, natives of nearby Red Banks, had relocated to St. Louis and opened a shoe factory. With a combination of drive, business smarts, and the U.S. government's need for thousands of army boots during the Spanish-American War, the Johnsons were soon financially flush. Oscar and his wife, Irene, built a fabulous estate west of St. Louis and kept Walter Place as their summer house and hunting lodge. Private trains, packed with friends in opulent Pullman cars, chugged from Missouri to Mississippi on a regular basis, and Walter Place gained a reputation as the social center of Holly Springs.

In the first years of the twentieth century, Johnson hired St. Louis architect Theodore Link, creator of Union Station, to remodel Walter Place. Link had already built the state's New Capitol and was hailed as one of the

nation's premier architects. He ripped out Walter Place's curving stair, replacing it with an "open arms" design, and substituted a small classical balcony for the old wrought-iron one which stretched across the façade.

While work was going on inside the mansion, Oscar Johnson turned his attention to the grounds. If he was going to have one of the finest houses in Mississippi, no ordinary garden and lawns would do. A German landscape architect was brought in, settled in a small house at the rear edge of the property, and supplied with no fewer than seventeen Japanese gardeners. A master plan, carefully drawn with india ink on linen, delineated the scope of the project. Thousands of native and exotic shrubs, flowers, and trees were brought in. Ponds were dug, drains sunk, waterfalls created, and roadways intertwined around the property. An arched Japanese bridge overlooked a fish pond, and plans were laid for a massive semicircular pergola. A reflecting pond on the west side of the house was located to capture the mansion's image in its waters.

Oscar Johnson was a generous man, and his intention was to deed the park to the people of Holly Springs. But

his legendary girth and exuberant lifestyle caught up with him before the park could be completed, and he died at age fifty-one in 1916, with his dream only partially finished.

Irene Johnson had no heart to finish Johnson Park or maintain the mansion. She sold Walter Place to local Ford dealer M. A. Greene in 1918, and it seemed that the Walter family's ties to the old house were gone forever. The vast gardens were subdivided for residential development, and gradually, over the next sixty years, all the hard work of the Japanese gardeners vanished. Privet hedges grew wild, wisteria vines twisted into cords several inches thick, and kudzu crept over the benches and pagodas.

The surviving Walter children, distressed at the decline of the house and grounds, bought it back at a sheriff's auction in 1934, paying four thousand dollars for the entire estate. It was occupied chiefly by caretakers for several

Left: Lost for almost a century, the foliage and flowers of Walter Place are being reclaimed.

Right: Thousands of shrubs bloom along walkways and amid pergolas, pagodas, and bridges.

decades, and the gardens were all but forgotten. The mansion was still a fabulous site for parties and social events, and many of the children of Holly Springs grew up with fond memories of teas on the lawn and swimming in the backyard pool.

One of those children was Jorja Swaney Lynn, who turned an adolescent dream of owning Walter Place into reality in 1983. She and her husband, Mike Lynn, were familiar with the tales of the vanished gardens, but had their hands full restoring the mansion to its former glory and making it livable for their family. The prospect of clearing out six decades' worth of snake-infested kudzu was just too daunting.

The reappearance of Theodore Link's original plat was the impetus for restoring Johnson Park. A neighbor had found the drawing in a pile of trash in the 1950s, and, unaware of its significance, had kept it for years before returning it to the Lynns. Armed with Link's inspiration and a small battalion of workers, the Lynns began the arduous task of reclaiming the gardens. As the out-of-control vegetation was stripped away, brick fish ponds, the Japanese bridge's pillars, and the ancient clay drains reemerged. Johnson Park was coming to life again.

Walter Place's gardens are being restored in several phases. Those that have been completed include waterfalls, a serpentine raised walkway through the woods, a Japanese pagoda, and steps of Arkansas fieldstone. When finished, it will rival the fabled gardens of the South, a natural sanctuary restored to its century-old glory.

Left: The original plat for Walter Place's gardens was recovered and is being used to re-create the site.

Right: Statuary, reflecting ponds, and the mansion itself complement the redevelopment of Oscar Johnson's gardens.

EUDORA WELTY HOUSE

In 1894, Lewis Fitzhugh opened a school for young ladies in his home on Jackson's Boyd Street. Two years later, it was destroyed by fire. Fitzhugh rebuilt on the same site and operated the college until his death in 1904. When fire once again destroyed the campus in 1910, the new owners moved the operation lock, stock, and barrel to the very northern edge of the rapidly expanding city. Belhaven College for Young Ladies settled on several heavily wooded acres near Asylum Heights and gave its name to the fashionable subdivision which grew up around it.

The streets of Belhaven were just being laid out with mules and oxen when Eudora Welty was a little girl living on Congress Street. Downtown Jackson and the New Capitol were her playgrounds, Davis School and the old Jackson Public Library her hideaways. In 1925, the year she turned sixteen, she could walk to Capitol Street to watch

the progress on the "skyscraper" which would house her father's company, Lamar Life Insurance. That was almost as exciting as hopping the streetcar to the end of North State Street and strolling a few blocks to Pinehurst Street, where the new Welty home was also under construction. She vividly recalled the anticipation of that year in *One Writer's Beginnings*: "It was a crowning year in [my father's] life. At the same time the new building [Lamar Life] was going up, so was our new house, designed by the same architect. The house was on a slight hill (my mother never could see the hill) covered with its original forest pines, on a gravel road then a little out from town, and was built in a style very much of its day, of stucco and brick and beams in the Tudor style."[76]

That house on Pinehurst would be Miss Welty's home for the rest of her long and celebrated life. In the high-ceilinged rooms, only two of which were air-conditinoed during her lifetime, she turned out prize-winning short stories, novels, and book reviews. Her mother, who lived

Eudora Welty's father moved his family to Belhaven when it was an outlying suburb of Jackson.

there with her until her death in 1966, was a talented horti-culturist, transforming the backyard into a wonderland of honeysuckle, pansies, azaleas, dogwoods, and spireas.

The house itself is a two-story Tudor Revival with brick veneer, stucco, and false half-timbering typical of the style. It features an irregular roofline with crossed gables and varied size windows. The interior is functional and comfortable, with a breakfast room, a parlor, living room, dining room, kitchen, and a downstairs bedroom with bath. The second floor consists only of two bedrooms and a bath, with a sleeping porch off one bedroom. Miss Welty's bedroom occupied the east side of the upper floor, and it was here that she did most of her writing. Her desk still sits by the triple windows overlooking the front yard.

Except for time spent away at college and brief stints in New York City and Europe, Miss Welty lived on the shady Pinehurst lot, first with her mother, and later alone, crafting the novels and stories which made her world famous. Her first short story was published in 1936 and her first book, *A Curtain of Green*, five years later. Positive

Left: Eudora Welty's mother filled their back garden with daylilies, pansies, honeysuckle vines, and azaleas.

Right: The Welty gardens and outdoor structures have been faithfully restored and preserved.

reviews poured in, and she would eventually be awarded a Guggenheim Fellowship and a Pulitzer Prize, among countless other honors.

Despite the accolades and awards, Miss Welty was not tempted to leave her homestead across from Belhaven College, despite the death of her mother and brothers. At age seventy-five, she reflected, "Living here's very pleasant. I like being in the house where nobody else has ever lived but my own family, even though it's lonely being the only person left. But I have never felt lonely here—perhaps it should be lonely. I live all over the house. It was built for a family—all the rooms open into something else and you don't feel shut off. It's not nearly as quiet as it was when we moved out here, when we had Rural Free Delivery with our mail and little wooden bridges crossing a creek down there that now has been concreted over. It was different, but I still like it. Jackson has grown up far beyond here, but we are a sort of little enclave where there hasn't been much change in this neighborhood."[77]

Novelist Anne Tyler visited with Miss Welty in 1980 and was taken with the atmosphere of the home and its gracious hostess.

> [W]hen her father, a country boy from Ohio, built his family a house back in 1925, he chose a spot near Belhaven College so he'd be sure to keep a bit of

green around them . . . [The] street is shaded by tall trees. Her driveway is a sheet of pine needles, and her house is dark and cool, with high ceilings, polished floors, comfortable furniture and a wonderfully stark old kitchen. She has lived here since she was in high school (and lived in Jackson all her life). Now she is alone, the last of a family of five. She loves the house, she says, but worries that she won't be able to keep it up properly: A porch she screened with $44 from the *Southern Review*, during the Depression, needs screening once again for a price so high that she has simply closed it off. One corner of the foundation has had to be rescued from sinking into the clay, which she describes as "shifting about like an elephant's hide."[78]

That screened porch had been ripped open by the tailwinds of Hurricane Camille eleven years prior to Anne Tyler's visit. It was just one example of the toll that time and Yazoo clay took on the Welty house before Miss Welty died in 2001. Knowing that her home was a literary treasure, and in keeping with her innate generosity, she had arranged for the Mississippi Department of Archives and History to take possession of the house and its contents after her death. Extensive foundation repairs and replacement of seventy-five-year-old electrical and plumbing systems were undertaken, and the house is now open for tours.

TISHOMINGO SWINGING BRIDGE

Two hundred and fifty million years ago, powerful geologic forces carved the Appalachian Mountains out of what would one day be the southeastern United States. Nature's upheaval left monumental boulders and craggy rock formations scattered about like giant Ping-Pong balls. Rivers and streams coursed through softer sandstone formations, digging gorges and meandering into the beds that they still occupy today.

Mississippi's connection to these ancient changes is viewed most dramatically in the far northeastern corner of the state. On the Natchez Trace above Tupelo, the scenery gradually alters until it resembles nothing else in the state. The hills are markedly more pronounced, and sharp outcroppings of dark stone pierce the roadside elevations. Caves and waterfalls are found in abundance, and the atmosphere seems thousands of miles from the gentle rolling landscape of central Mississippi or the endless flat vistas of the Delta.

The same geologic oddities that are responsible for the dramatic scenery of Tishomingo County also rendered the land useless for most crops. When the Great Depression descended on America in the early 1930s, it hit this corner of Mississippi especially hard. Over one million acres of the state's twenty-nine million had been seized for delinquent taxes, and President Roosevelt's administration was eager to put that idle land to use creating jobs. When Roosevelt signed the Civilian Conservation Corps bill, Mississippi was primed and enthusiastic. The Jackson *Clarion-Ledger* predicted that "[It] is the plan of Mississippi to be right under the apple when it falls."[79] At least a portion of those million acres could be immediately utilized, bringing CCC jobs to young men with no other prospects.

In 1934, the Mississippi legislature signed off on House Bill #446, which established the state park system. Within a year, Leroy Percy State Park, near Hollandale, was ready

Tishomingo State Park's swinging bridge utilizes the same engineering principles as the Golden Gate Bridge and the Brooklyn Bridge.

for business. By 1937, thirty-four CCC camps were operational across Mississippi, employing almost ten thousand men. Their efforts would pull $60 million in federal funds into the nation's poorest state. Even more crucial for the future was that the program would result in the planting of 147,000,000 trees and 2,000 miles of new roads.

Many of those trees and roads were incorporated into the state park system, which originally included ten sites and over ten thousand acres. The parks were scattered from the Gulf Coast to the Tennessee line, utilizing natural features in their buildings, campgrounds, and lakes. None featured such dramatic topography as Tishomingo State Park. Situated close to Woodall Mountain, the highest elevation in the state, Tishomingo featured steep hillsides, dense forests, and the languid, winding Bear Creek. The entire park was geared to outdoor recreation. A 1936 landscape architect's report painted an optimistic picture: "This is one park in Mississippi where the trails will be popular, as the public has already proved that it is exceedingly fond of walking among the rocks and small caves and along the rim of the gorge. Two rather large foot bridges will be necessary to provide access to both sides of the creek. Cost of both 1000–1500 man days. About four miles of trails will be desirable and should require about 400 man days."[80]

Tishomingo State Park would acquire thirteen miles of trails, winding through some of the most impressive scenery in Mississippi, along and above both sides of Bear

Top: Blocks of sandstone carved from the park's hillsides anchor the bridge's cables.

Bottom: A Prentiss County pioneer cabin was an appropriate addition to Tishomingo State Park.

Creek. The need was apparent to link the more developed side of the creek, with its lodges, cabins, and swimming pool, to the natural side. A simple footbridge would have sufficed, but some long-forgotten CCC man came up with a more inspired idea. A swinging bridge was designed that would use steel cables discarded after the completion of Pickwick Dam. It utilized, in miniature, the same technology as the Brooklyn Bridge and the Golden Gate Bridge. Blocks of sandstone, quarried in the park, were fashioned into archways at each end of the bridge. Cables were spliced and strung in graceful arches high above Bear Creek. Wooden planks were laid down for a walkway that provides just enough spring to make the crossing exciting.

Tishomingo's 1,530 acres officially opened in May 1939, and it has closed only during World War II, when its facilities were reserved for the use of military personnel. Over those seven decades, thousands have canoed Bear Creek, hiked the forests, and swung precariously over the water on the delightful swinging bridge.

NOTES

1. Andre Penicaut, as quoted in David Sansing, Sim C. Callon, and Carolyn Vance Smith, *Natchez: An Illustrated History* (Natchez: Plantation Publishing Company, 1992), 12.

2. Mrs. Edmund Noel, as quoted in Robert Milton Winter, *Shadow of a Mighty Rock: A Social and Cultural History of Presbyterianism in Marshall County, Mississippi* (Franklin, TN: Providence House Publishers, 1997), 395.

3. W. C. C. Claiborne, as quoted in Sansing, Callon, and Smith, *Natchez: An Illustrated History*, 103.

4. Eliza Quitman, as quoted in Robert E. May, *John A. Quitman: Old South Crusader* (Baton Rouge: Louisiana State University Press, 1985), 137.

5. Daniel Barringer, as quoted in May, *John A. Quitman*, 138.

6. Hosea W. Rood, as quoted in May, *John A. Quitman*, 353.

7. George Poindexter, as quoted in *Mississippi: The Official and Statistical Register 1912* (Nashville: Press of Brandon Printing Company, 1912), 284.

8. Stark Young, *So Red the Rose* (New York: Charles Scribner's Sons, 1934).

9. Carlton Jonathan Corliss, *Main Line of Mid-America: The Story of the Illinois Central* (New York: Creative Age Press, 1950), 259.

10. Advertisement in *Vicksburg Weekly Whig*, December 5, 1849, as quoted in Terrence J. Winschel, *Alice Shirley and the Story of Wexford Lodge* (n.p.: Eastern National Press, 1997), 4.

11. Alice Shirley Eaton, as quoted in Winschel, *Alice Shirley*, 10.

12. Ibid.

13. Ibid., 11–12.

14. Ibid., 16.

15. Ibid., 21.

16. Ibid., 22.

17. *Mississippi Senate Journal*, 1836, 217.

18. *Southern Sun*, December 15, 1838.

19. Major J. W. Kennedy, as quoted by Katy Headley in *Claiborne County, Mississippi: The Promised Land* (Port Gibson: Claiborne Historical Society, 1976), 170.

20. *Port Gibson Correspondent*, October 14, 1837.

21. *Natchez Free Trader*, April 17, 1845.

22. Kennedy, as quoted in Headley, *Claiborne County, Mississippi*, 171.

23. Mrs. Benjamin Humphreys, as quoted by Lizzie George Henderson, "Private Letters of Mrs. Humphreys, Written Immediately Before and After the Ejection of Her Husband from the Executive Mansion," *Publications of the Mississippi Historical Society* 3 (1900), 99–106.

24. Ibid.

25. Ibid.

26. James K. Vardaman, as quoted in David Sansing and Carroll Waller, *A History of the Mississippi Governor's Mansion* (Jackson: University Press of Mississippi, 1977), 100.

27. Frank Abbott Jones, unpublished manuscript in the collection of Joe Schmelzer, 1998.

28. Ibid.

29. Commissioners' Report to the General Assembly, November 20, 1821.

30. *Frank Leslie's Illustrated Newspaper*, October 17, 1865.

31. *Freemasons Monthly Magazine*, December 1847.

32. Robert Morris, as quoted from his diary, in the files of the Mississippi Department of Archives and History.

33. Ibid.

34. *The WPA Guide to the Magnolia State* (Jackson: University Press of Mississippi, 1988), 386.

35. John Newton Waddel, *Memorials of Academic Life* (Richmond, 1891), 262, as cited in Allen Cabaniss, *The University of Mississippi: Its First Hundred Years* (Jackson: University Press of Mississippi, 1971), 9.

36. Hugh Clegg, as quoted in David Sansing, *The University of Mississippi: A Sesquicentennial History* (Jackson: University Press of Mississippi, 1999), 303.

37. Willie Morris, as quoted in Sansing, *University of Mississippi*, 303.

38. Mary Reynolds, as quoted in M. James Stevens, "Biloxi's First Lady Light House Keeper," *Journal of Mississippi History* 36 (February 1974), 39–42.

39. William Mercer Green, as quoted in his journal, July 19, 1852.

40. Hugh Miller Thompson II, *The Johnstones of Annandale* (self-published, 1992), 42.

41. Ibid., 42–44.

42. William Mercer Green, as quoted in Thompson, *Johnstones*, 15.

43. Pat DeWeese, as quoted by Lynn Watkins in the Jackson *Clarion-Ledger*, "Rural Gothic Cottage Can Be Viewed," October 29, 1978.

44. L. Q. C. Lamar, as quoted by Frank Johnston, "The Conference of October 15th, 1875, Between General George and Governor Ames," *Publications of the Mississippi Historical Society* 6 (1902): 65–77.

45. Mildred Spurrier Topp, *Smile Please* (Cambridge: The Riverside Press, 1948).

46. Lewis Harper, *Preliminary Report on the Geology and Agriculture of the State of Mississippi*, 1857, 320.

47. *Journal of the Proceedings of the Twenty-Second Annual Convention of the Protestant Episcopal Church of the Diocese of Mississippi*, May 10, 1848, 12.

48. William Mercer Green, journal entry, 1855, 25–26.

49. William Mercer Green, as quoted by Sandra Lee McIntire, "St. John's History Shows Rise, Fall of Plantation Life," *Delta Democrat Times*, October 26, 1992.

50. John Falkner, *My Brother Bill* (New York: Trident Press, 1963), 14–15.

51. Murry Falkner, *The Falkners of Mississippi* (Baton Rouge: Louisiana State University Press, 1967), 12–13.

52. Ibid., 20.

53. Dunbar Rowland, *Mississippi* (Spartanburg: The Reprint Company, 1976), 352.

54. Owen Van Vacter, writing in *The Commonwealth*, January 2, 1858, as quoted by Laura Bowers, *Madison County Herald*, March 27, 1975.

55. James H. Otey, as quoted in Elmo Howell, *Mississippi Back Roads* (n.p., n.d.), 65.

56. Christ Episcopal Church Vestry minutes, November 17, 1856.

57. William Mercer Green, as quoted by Mary Warren Miller, "Tour of Church Hill," unpublished tour guide, 1993, 36.

58. James S. Johnson, as quoted in Howell, *Mississippi Back Roads*, 66.

59. Mary Loughborough, as quoted in Gordon Cotton, *Vicksburg: Southern Stories of the Siege* (self-published, 1988).

60. *Southern Reveille*, February 21, 1890.

61. Smith C. Daniell IV, as told to L. Harrell, files of the Mississippi Department of Archives and History, 1963.

62. George Poindexter, as quoted in *Mississippi: The Official and Statistical Register 1912*, 284.

63. Alice Shirley Eaton, as quoted in Winschel, *Alice Shirley*, 10.

64. *Southwestern*, November 9, 1871, as quoted in Headley, *Claiborne County, Mississippi*, 133.

65. Quotation from unnamed source in "Cumberlands Once Prominent Church; Progressed from Log Cabin to Brick," *Oxford Eagle*, August 22, 1957.

66. Eunice Darby Grubbs, as quoted in Steven H. Stubbs, *Mississippi's Giant Houseparty: The History of the Neshoba County Fair* (Philadelphia: Dancing Rabbit Press, 2005), 51.

67. Ronald Reagan, as quoted in Stubbs, *Mississippi's Giant Houseparty*, 448.

68. *Port Gibson Reveille*, November 18, 1891.

69. Ibid., February 20, 1902.

70. Ibid., February 27, 1902.

71. Excerpts from the diary of Private Jackman, private collection.

72. *Minutes of the City of Jackson*, Book J., 1904, 87–88.

73. Contract between United Daughters of the Confederacy and Columbus Marble Works, September 18, 1912.

74. James K. Vardaman, as quoted in Christopher Waldrep, *Vicksburg's Long Shadow* (Lanham: Rowman & Littlefield Publishers, 2005), 180.

75. Horace Greeley Austin, as told to Sara Gwin Kelsh, undated manuscript in the author's collection.

76. Eudora Welty, *One Writer's Beginnings* (New York: Warner Books, 1991), 90.

77. Eudora Welty, as quoted by Patricia Wheatley, "Eudora Welty: A Writer's Beginnings," in Peggy Whitman Prenshaw, ed., *More Conversations with Eudora Welty* (Jackson: University Press of Mississippi, 1996), 121–22.

78. Anne Tyler, as quoted in "A Visit with Eudora Welty," *New York Times Book Review*, November 2, 1980, 33–34. Reprinted in Prenshaw, ed., *More Conversations*, 69.

79. Jackson *Clarion-Ledger*, March 31, 1933.

80. Graham Rushton, "Report on Formulation of Future Work Programs Miss-SP-5-Tishomingo," December 9, 1936.

BIBLIOGRAPHY

Note: Each National Register of Historic Places site has a nomination form and information file in the Historic Preservation Division of the Mississippi Department of Archives and History. These are not listed separately in this bibliography, although they were utilized extensively.

Anderson, Helen Craft. "A Chapter in the Yellow Fever Epidemic of 1878." *Publications of the Mississippi Historical Society* 10 (1909): 223–36.

Austin, Horace Greeley. Undated, unpublished manuscript of interview by Sara Kelsh.

Bailey, Eileen. "Victoria: Once-condemned Aberdeen Home Turned Into Showplace." *Northeast Mississippi Daily Journal*, March 3, 1996.

Bettersworth, John K. *Confederate Mississippi: The People and Policies of a Cotton State in Wartime*. Philadelphia: Porcupine Press, 1978.

Brinson, Carroll. *Jackson: A Special Kind of Place*. Jackson, Miss.: City of Jackson, 1977.

Brough, Charles Hillman. "Historic Clinton." *Publications of the Mississippi Historical Society* 7 (1903): 281–311.

Burger, Nash K. "Adam Cloud, Mississippi's First Episcopal Clergyman." *Journal of Mississippi History* 9 (January): 88–97.

Cabaniss, Allen. *The University of Mississippi: Its First Hundred Years*. Jackson: University Press of Mississippi, 1971.

Cain, Helen, and Anne D. Czarniecki. *An Illustrated Guide to the Mississippi Governor's Mansion*. Jackson: University Press of Mississippi, 1984.

Clayton, Claude F. "The Dedication of the Last Courthouse of Old Tishomingo County at Jacinto, Mississippi." *Journal of Mississippi History* 31 (1969): 172–86.

Crocker, Brad. "Roths Make Longfellow a Residence for First Time Since 1938." *The Mississippi Press*, June 10, 2006.

Crocker, Mary Wallace. *Historic Architecture in Mississippi*. Jackson: University Press of Mississippi, 1973.

Daniell, Smith C., IV. "Windsor." Unpublished manuscript in Mississippi Department of Archives and History files, 1963.

Daniels, Jonathan. *The Devil's Backbone*. New York: McGraw-Hill Publishing Co., 1962.

Deupree, J. G. "The Capture of Holly Springs, Ms., December 20, 1862." *Publications of the Mississippi Historical Society* 4 (1901): 49–61.

Douglas, Ed Polk. *Architecture in Claiborne County, Mississippi*. Jackson: Mississippi Department of Archives and History, 1974.

Doyle, Don H. *Faulkner's County: The Historical Roots of Yoknapatawpha*. Chapel Hill: University of North Carolina Press, 2001.

Eaddy, Justin C. "Mississippi's State Parks: The New Deal's Mixed Legacy." *Journal of Mississippi History* 45 (Summer 2003): 147–168.

Fearn, Anne Walter. *My Days of Strength*. New York: Harper & Brothers, 1939.

Finley, Lori. *Traveling the Natchez Trace*. Winston-Salem: Blair Publishing Co., 1995.

Fortune, Porter L., Jr. "The Formative Period." Chapter 10 in *A History of Mississippi*, edited by Richard A. McLemore. Jackson: University Press of Mississippi, 1973.

Graham, Charlotte. "Rectory Returns to Chapel of the Cross after 135 Years." Jackson *Clarion-Ledger*, September 9, 2000.

Greaves, Linda T., Lois Smith Clover, Preston Myers Hays, and Elizabeth Wise Copeland. *Jackson Landmarks*. Jackson: Junior League of Jackson, 1982.

Gurney, Bill. *Mississippi Courthouses: Then and Now*. Fulton, MS: Itawamba County Times, 1987.

Halsell, Willie D. "Migration and Settlement into Leflore County, 1833–1876." *Journal of Mississippi History* 10 (1948): 240–60.

Hartje, Robert G. *Van Dorn: The Life and Times of a Confederate General*. Nashville: Vanderbilt University Press, 1967.

Headley, Katy M. *Claiborne County, Mississippi: The Promised Land*. Port Gibson: Claiborne County Historical Society, 1976.

Hines, Thomas S. *William Faulkner and the Tangible Past*. Berkeley: University of California Press, 1996.

Howell, Elmo. *Mississippi Back Roads*. N.p., n.d.

———. *Mississippi Scenes*. N.p., n.d.

Jamison, Lena Mitchell. "The Natchez Trace: A Federal Highway of the Old Southwest." *Journal of Mississippi History* 1 (1939): 82–99.

Johnston, Frank. "The Conference of October 15th, 1875, Between General George and Governor Ames." *Publications of the Mississippi Historical Society* 6 (1902): 65–77.

Jones, Frank Abbott. "Clifton." Unpublished manuscript dated April 1998, in the collection of Joe Schmelzer.

Kane, Harnett. *Natchez on the Mississippi*. New York: William Morrow and Company, 1947.

Lucas, Aubrey K. "Education in Mississippi from Statehood to the Civil War." Chapter 13 in *A History of Mississippi*, edited by Richard A. McLemore. Jackson: University Press of Mississippi, 1973.

Marshall, Theodora Britton, and Gladys Crail Evans. *They Found It in Natchez*. New Orleans: Pelican Press, 1939.

May, Robert E. *John A. Quitman: Old South Crusader*. Baton Rouge: Louisiana State University Press, 1985.

McAlexander, H. H. *Southern Tapestry*. Virginia Beach: Donning Publishing Company, 2000.

McCain, William D. *The Story of Jackson*. Jackson: J. F. Hyer Publishing, 1953.

McGinnis, Helen. *Hiking Mississippi: A Guide to Trails and Natural Areas*. Jackson: University Press of Mississippi, 1994.

McLemore, Richard A. *A History of Mississippi Baptists*. Jackson: Mississippi Baptist Convention Board, 1971.

Mead, Carol Lynn. *The Land Between Two Rivers*. Canton: Friends of the Madison County/Canton Public Library, 1987.

Miller, Mary Warren, Ronald W. Miller, and David King Gleason. *The Great Houses of Natchez*. Jackson: University Press of Mississippi, 1986.

Mississippi Industrial College catalogue, 1940–1941.

Moore, John Hebron. *The Emergence of the Cotton Kingdom in the Old Southwest*. Baton Rouge: Louisiana State University Press, 1988.

Polk, Noel, ed. *Natchez Before 1830*. Jackson: University Press of Mississippi, 1989.

Ragusin, Anthony V. "The Centennial of the Biloxi Lighthouse." *Journal of Mississippi History* 11 (January 1949): 204–6.

Revels, James G. "Redeemers, Rednecks and Racial Integrity." Chapter 20 in *A History of Mississippi*, edited by Richard A. McLemore. Jackson: University Press of Mississippi, 1973.

Rowland, Dunbar. *Mississippi*. 2 vols. 1907. Spartanburg: The Reprint Company, 1976.

Sansing, David G. "Congressional Reconstruction." Chapter 19 in *A History of Mississippi*, edited by Richard A. McLemore. Jackson: University Press of Mississippi, 1973.

———. "L. Q. C. Lamar." *Oxford-Lafayette County Heritage Foundation Newsletter*, n.d.

———. *Making Haste Slowly: The Troubled History of Higher Education in Mississippi*. Jackson: University Press of Mississippi, 1990.

———. *The University of Mississippi: A Sesquicentennial History*. Jackson: University Press of Mississippi, 1999.

Sansing, David G., Sim C. Callon, and Carolyn Vance Smith. *Natchez: An Illustrated History*. Natchez: Plantation Publishing Company, 1992.

Sansing, David G., and Carroll Waller. *A History of the Mississippi Governor's Mansion*. Jackson: University Press of Mississippi, 1977.

Scarborough, William K. "Heartland of the Cotton Kingdom." Chapter 12 in *A History of Mississippi*, edited by Richard A. McLemore. Jackson: University Press of Mississippi, 1973.

Skates, John Ray. *Mississippi's Old Capitol: Biography of a Building*. Jackson: Mississippi Department of Archives and History, 1990.

Smith, J. Frazer. *White Pillars: The Architecture of the South*. New York: Bramhall House, 1941.

Stevens, M. James. "Biloxi's First Lady Light House Keeper." *Journal of Mississippi History* 36 (February 1974): 39–42.

Stubbs, Steven H. *Mississippi's Giant Houseparty: The History of the Neshoba County Fair*. Philadelphia: Dancing Rabbit Press, 2005.

Tallo, LaJuan. "Mississippi's Courthouses: Tate County Courthouse." *The Mississippi Lawyer* (March–April 2001): 28–29.

Thompson, Hugh Miller, II. *The Johnstones of Annandale*. N.p., 1992.

Turitz, Leo E., and Evelyn Turitz. *Jews in Early Mississippi*. Jackson: University Press of Mississippi, 1983.

Waldrep, Christopher. *Vicksburg's Long Shadow*. Lanham: Bowman and Littlefield, 2005.

Website for Our Lady of the Gulf Catholic Church. www.olg church.net/history/htm.

Welty, Eudora. *One Writer's Beginnings*. New York: Warner Books, 1991.

Wheatley, Patricia. "Eudora Welty: A Writer's Beginnings." In *More Conversations with Eudora Welty*, edited by Peggy Whitman Prenshaw. Jackson: University Press of Mississippi, 1996.

Williamson, Joel. *William Faulkner and Southern History*. New York: Oxford University Press, 1993.

Wilson, Jack Case. *Faulkners, Fortunes and Flames*. Nashville: Annandale Press, n.d.

Winschel, Terrence J. *Alice Shirley and the Story of Wexford Lodge*. N.p.: Eastern National Press, 1993.

Winter, Robert Milton. *Shadow of a Mighty Rock: A Social and Cultural History of Presbyterianism in Marshall County, Mississippi*. Franklin, TN: Providence House Publishers, 1997.

Works Progress Administration. *Mississippi: The WPA Guide to the Magnolia State*. 1938. Reprint, Jackson: University Press of Mississippi, 1988.

Index